IN THE SHADOW OF CLAUDE

In the Shadow of Claude

MEMORIES OF A BEDFORDSHIRE FARMER

CLAUDE BANKS

PENNY YOUNG

Matador
Unit E2 Airfield Business Park,
Harrison Road, Market Harborough,
Leicestershire. LE16 7UL
Tel: 0116 2792299
Email: books@troubador.co.uk
Web: www.troubador.co.uk/matador
Twitter: @matadorbooks

ISBN 978 180313 5731

British Library Cataloguing in Publication Data.
A catalogue record for this book is available from the British Library.

Printed and bound in the UK by TJ Books Limited, Padstow, Cornwall
Typeset in 11pt Aldine401 BT by Troubador Publishing Ltd, Leicester, UK

Matador is an imprint of Troubador Publishing Ltd

I dedicate this book to my sister, Sally. In 2019, just two years after losing Dad, I was diagnosed with breast cancer. My sister told me right from the start, 'We will fight this thing together, you are not on your own, I will be with you every step of the way'. I cannot tell you how much this meant, and my sister was true to her word, and I could not have done it without her. I am pleased to say that I am now in remission.

In Memory of
Joyce Shrubbs 1927 – 2021
Mary Roddis 1929 – 2017
Bob Banks 1930 – 2022

Contents

World War 2 – Claude's Version of Events!

Sport

The Villages and its Characters

Foreword

Just as it seemed that the 'well of stories' had run dry some previously unseen tracts turned up and they form the core of the current volume. Reading them is like meeting up again with an old friend. Claude's eye for detail and the quality of the writing remains as high as ever. His literary faculties remained undimmed until his death some 5 years ago.

A lifelong farmer around Pertenhall his early life was hard and subject to the vagaries of all small farmers; economic depression, falling incomes, rising costs, uncertain markets etc. The 'can and make do' attitude of that generation percolates through many of the stories. The descriptions of the state of farming between the World Wars, when it was in an economic wilderness, is enthralling. How would we have coped as modern individuals I wondered?

Life was certainly spiced up by the presence of the American Forces in the 1940s. They certainly knew how to party and so did Claude when he spent three or four days in London for VE-day, entering into the swing of things! Two favourite accounts I found gripping. Firstly – a school history lesson was aborted as the prescient teacher said, "History is being made today as German forces speed across France at the pace of a motor bike. None knows where matters will end". Secondly – like all lads of 17, when Claude tried to enlist, the recruiting officer, upon learning of his farming profession, turned him down. In January 1943 he was told the Country only had three weeks of food supplies remaining – so go home and plough for England! Spirits were instantly raised.

Claude's detailed farm diaries for the 1950s and 60s proved to be mines of information for Penny's adaptations. Each one a treasure trove and these form the basis of being mini farming tutorials – covering agricultural terms, crop rotations, farming practices, economics and much more. We learn such a lot from them.

We learn too about some of yesteryears local heritage features (some of which could easily be restored) on or near to his land at the time. Two especially caught the eye, the 'footprints' of the old point-to-point racecourse, a big event in its day, at the birth of the 20th Century. Claude could still see parts of existing hedges which were prepared as jumps. The Chadwell Spring and it's healing waters are featured. Sadly, today it is suffused into a large bramble patch. This could be a wonderful opportunity for rehabilitation and for the recreation or restoration of an old standpipe with its chained metal cup. This must have quenched the thirst of many a farmworker or passer-by. They would be regarded as local heritage features, alongside a visible source of spring water.

Particular mention must be made of Claude's daughter and co-author Penny Young. Her contributions remain largely unseen. However, Penny has supervised and managed all the steps from typing his stories to the production of all three books. Her guiding, unseen hand is evident on every page. She has similar values, insights, and a writing style to her father's. Penny continues to publish monthly stories – many involving Claude, in 'The Bystander' and is developing a cult following of her own, as she emerges from being in 'the shadow of Claude' and continuing to document features and life in and around Kimbolton.

There is a strong story telling bond between father and daughter as they have striven to publicise Claude's life and events to a wider audience. They could not have done any better. Undoubtedly he was and still remains her main 'paragon' in life.

Dr. Gareth Thomas.

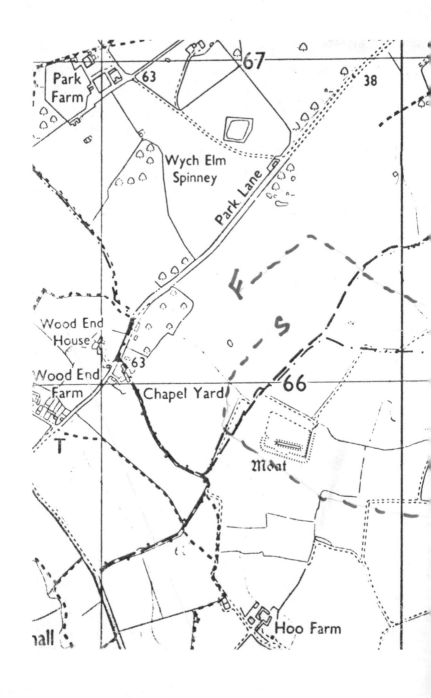

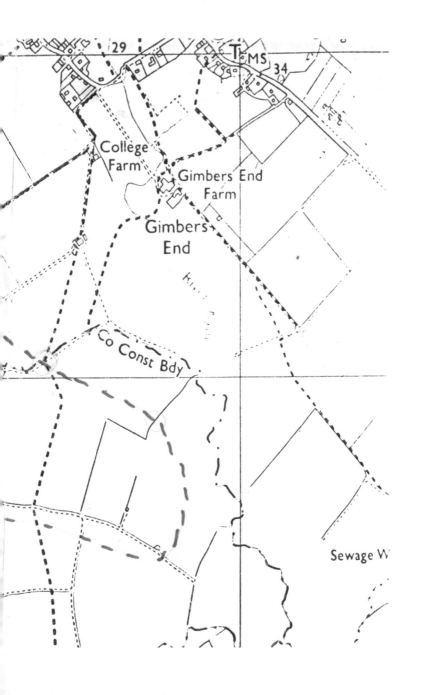

Introduction

Following the publication of "Once a Man – Twice a Boy" in 2014 and "After You Claude" in 2016, Dad continued writing his monthly stories for "The Bystander", right up until his death at the age of 91 in February 2017. The publisher of the magazine asked me if I thought I could continue to write a monthly article, as the readers enjoyed the stories so much. I said that I would 'give it a go' and here we are, five years after losing Dad – Claude, and the production line has not run dry!

Friends and family were beginning to remark that, "surely you must have enough stories for another book by now", but I felt that something was still missing. Two 'eureka' moments came within a short space of time and a month later, the book was born. Two stashes of Dad's unseen stories were unearthed and whilst some of the tales of Dad's early life will have featured in his first two books, his wonderful story telling often includes new anecdotes which haven't seen the light of day before and are definitely worth another outing.

Dad had long wanted to write the story of the Racecourse and indeed his research for it goes back to 1994, well before he had taken up his second career as an author!

I am particularly pleased that I discovered the fat envelope of newspaper cuttings, race cards and correspondence, with various people from Birmingham to Lockerbie in Scotland helping with Claude's research. How did he even know these people? I will never know, but crucially, the envelope included a Map of Pertenhall and Stonely and, hand-drawn by Dad, the route the races took over "The Hoo Course", which bisects both villages and which are at the heart of all dad's stories. This was the final missing piece of the jigsaw, and I am delighted to give you – "In the Shadow of Claude".

I am thrilled with the book and so proud of my Dad, his lust for life, even up to the very end, and I hear his voice on every page and he will always be with me.

Every Picture Tells a Story

On the front cover we see Claude, sitting on a bench outside Kimbolton Castle for 'Old Kimboltonians Day' in 2014, where he had kindly been given permission by the headmaster to launch his first book 'Once a Man – Twice a Boy'. We had ordered 800 copies of the book and the boxes of books filled my dining room. On this first day, I think we sold 30 copies – one box full! I must admit, I was panicking somewhat, but suddenly, the sale of books took off, and we ended up having to have a second print run of 300 books and these also sold out.

On the back cover, we see Claude, with Henry, great-grandson, mentioned in the story, 'Sportsday'.

The Map of the Racecourse – this was the key to the whole book coming together. You can see annotated by Claude 'S' for the start and 'F' for the finish of the race. The majority of Claude's life was lived within the confines of this Map, and you will see references to 'Hoo Farm' and 'College Farm'.

CHAPTER ONE

Early Life

Claude's Early Life

The first thing I can remember happening was being put to bed by my grandmother, in one of the many bedrooms in the large farmhouse, known as Manor Farm, Pertenhall. As she tucked me in, I can remember the pillow was soft and inviting and as she sang several verses of 'Twinkle twinkle little Star', I fell fast asleep. I presume Grandma went downstairs to discuss the unfortunate events that had happened earlier in the day with her daughter, Aunt Amy and perhaps with Grandfather. Later in life I became aware that fateful day, which was Boxing Day, 1928, my mother had been found dead in somewhat unusual circumstances. Me and my elder sister Stancy were quickly taken up to Grandma's house and my younger sister Fay was fostered by some very good friends in the village, named Abrahams.

I don't suppose many women of 60 years of age would be too excited about having a two-year-old boy (I was one month off my third birthday), and a seven-year-old girl (six weeks off her eighth birthday), arrive unexpectedly on their doorstep, but of course Grandma's

Dad's beloved Grandmother Kate Banks (nee Reynolds) 1865 – 1944. We only have three photos of Kate, and the two better ones were used in the earlier books, but Claude's grandmother was such a huge influence on his early life, and I think moulded him into the character and person he became, and she had to be included in Claude's book.

are a breed apart, and as far as I can remember, things went quite smoothly.

Just what it was like in the Abraham household, having a nine-month-old baby girl taking up residence, was another matter.

Actually, similar upheavals were to happen around 10 years later, with evacuees being sent to the country villages from cities which were about to come under attack from the German Air force.

I cannot remember that much about Stancy being up at Manor Farm, maybe she went back to Chadwell Farm, which was our home, because eight-year-old girls can, and often do, jobs around the house and I am sure she would have tried to be useful and of course she would have been back to school, as soon as the Spring Term started.

Manor Farm was very extensive and had adjoining outbuildings, the guttering of which all led to the soft water tank outside of the back door. This soft water was most useful for doing the weekly wash and when the tank was getting full during a storm, Grandma would bale some of it out and put it into the copper, so none was wasted. The distance that some of this rainwater had to travel around the guttering, meant that it was still dripping into the tank long after it had stopped raining, but I was not allowed to go out and play until the spout had dried off, which disappointed me quite a lot.

Some days, Grandfather would take me for a ride around the farm in the pony and trap, which would give Grandma and Aunt Amy a break. I would be useful to open gates to let the pony go through, although if the gate was heavy and did not swing easily, Grandfather would do it and I drove the pony, not always successfully.

*

I started at Pertenhall School in the Easter Term, 1930, in the infants' class, taught by Miss Kate Cook, from Hoo Farm. She was a very kind lady, and our classroom was quite small, separated from the main classroom by a thick curtain. There was no electricity in Pertenhall at that time, so oil lamps were used, with coal fires to keep the place warm. Mrs Roddis would light the fire soon after seven in the morning and by the time the children arrived, it was quite snug. The water had to be fetched from next door,

3

where an old fellow named Mr Day lived. He was almost bent double with arthritis, but he was never grumpy like most old people used to be (and probably still are!)

I was taken to school that first day by Grandma in the pony and trap. We went via The Avenue, which seemed to me, at the time, the long way round, but looking back, I think she avoided going past Chadwell Farm, owing to the sad happening in the recent past. There is a photo of the infant class, taken in about June 1930 and it includes some of the youngsters from Swineshead, the neighbouring village. As the number of children in Swineshead were quite small, and Pertenhall not much better, the education authority decided that an amalgamation of the two schools would be the best proposition.

A bus, owned by Edgar Bayes from Kimbolton, called at Pertenhall at 8.15am and picked up all pupils aged 11 and over and then collected all the 11 and over's from Swineshead and they all went on to Risely for their day's education. The bus then called back at Swineshead, picking up the under 11's and brought them back to Pertenhall School by about 9am, ready to start school with the local children. In the afternoon, the process was reversed, with the school bus being one of a very few motor vehicles which used that road for a good many years, except for the one day in April every year, when the point-to-point races were held at Risely.

*

Before the start of the Autumn term in 1930, our Father had decided to take on Wakes Farm at Eversholt and no doubt it was a big upheaval moving everything a distance

4

of probably 30 odd miles and right through the centre of Bedford into the bargain.

Dad had by this time remarried and probably thought it best to get away from Chadwell Farm, although Grandfather continued to farm the land, as it adjoined Manor Farm. Stancy and I went to the local school at Eversholt, which was situated quite a long way from Wakes Farm, which had a drive of about half a mile, before you even reached the main road. Stancy cycled to and fro every day, with me on the carrier at the back, which must have given her good leg muscles! I cannot remember much about our education there, because after only a year, Dad must have got fed up with trying to earn a living off the very poor soil, that was infested with rabbits and returned to Chadwell Farm in the Autumn of 1931. The two things which stand out in my mind about Eversholt was, a couple of boys of my age at the school, I think their names were Jellis, had a distinctly odd look about them and I have heard since that they were, what is now known as, 'blue babies'. Quite what became of them, I know not. The second thing I remember, I had my lunch packed up to go into the hayfield with the workmen and one of them had a large onion to eat with his sandwiches. He gave me a large slice and I crunched it up in my mouth and it was so hot, it nearly blew the top of my head off, but I dare not spit it out, or I would have been called a sissy, so I suffered in silence, but learned a lesson into the bargain.

When Dad remarried, he employed a maidservant, named Maud Summerfield, from one of the homes in Bedford. She had a son who worked on the farm. She was very tall and thin and usually bad-tempered. I doubt if she

5

had had much of a life and the son was probably illegitimate, although there were plenty more about like that then, as there are now. This housemaid took quite a dislike to me and having been made such a fuss of by Grandma and Aunt Amy, I now came down to earth with quite a bump! A new stepmother, a meddlesome housemaid and a fairly spoilt five year old were not a good mixture, so the half mile up to Manor Farm posed no problem for my strong, though very short legs.

Another couple of terms in the infants' class was my next lot and one of the most vivid memories was Miss Cook bringing to school one morning, a half-crown and a two shilling piece that had been recovered from a thatched house fire, next to Hoo Farm, where Miss Cook lived. This thatched house was occupied by a Miss Dickens and her partner, (yes there were people who lived with partners in 1931), Joe Howe. The house caught alight and burned down one windy night, before the fire brigade could get to it. The coins had half melted and twisted into weird shapes before they cooled down.

*

I was spending more time at Grandma's than at home, for a number of reasons, one of which was that there were so many more boys to play with at that end of the village. Bob Roddis was my age and Jim Clark a bit older. Stanley and Fred Dawson were either side of my age and we all played cricket. Any spare time we had, we were straight into the cricket field, which was near the crossroads at Green End. I well remember when Grandma asked me what I would like for Christmas or my birthday, I would always ask for a cricket bat, or ball, or stumps or a scorebook. Once she said, "I can't make out why you are so mad on cricket, my boy". I replied, "One day Grandma, it won't be Bradman, it will be Banks"! Unfortunately, I did not reach this level of achievement, but the love of the game has burned brightly in me ever since and so many cricketers that I have played with, or against have become friends. I must say that I owe cricket a great debt of gratitude, although I have always tried to put as much back as I have taken out and still do to this day.

We often played home and away to the boys in Lt.Staughton and Keysoe and once, when going to Lt.Staughton, Gordon Abraham, who was the oldest and had a bicycle, ferried the younger ones all the way, taking one on the crossbar and another on the carrier, a mile or so, then coming back for two more of us. Then we all had to walk up the steep Spring Hill, before playing for a couple of hours in the grass field, behind where the new chapel is now.

At Keysoe, we played in a different field each time. No doubt the pitch was not always the best, but as long as we had an innings or two, no one seemed to bother. It was the game that counted, more than the result. The Keysoe team consisted of mainly Stapletons, this was a huge family with probably six or seven boys and a couple of girls. Jeff, Claude, Cliff, Stan and Oliver were some of them.

We also used to play cricket in the school playground, and it is a job to know what I would have done with my life, had cricket not been invented!

★

Pertenhall and Swineshead School, 1932 – 1933, 5 to 11 year olds

Back Row L-R *Sidney Shelton, Jim Clarke, John Mansfield, Albert Reynolds, Peter Roddis.*
Middle Row *John Shelton, Fred Braybrook, Stan Nicholson, Lucy Maclelland, Raymond Clarke, Frank Condliffe, Joan Peppit, Gladys Reynolds.*
Front Row *Douglas Stanton, Claude Banks, Pam Russell, Aubrey Clark, Michael Clark, Grace Nicholson, Bob Roddis, Muriel Clark, Margery Elliott, Robert Thomgate, Spencer Leflay*

In those days, the idea of school dinners had not been thought of, so a good many children took sandwiches for their lunch. I used to walk back to Grandma's (or run, more likely) for lunch and although it was a good mile each way, we thought nothing of that. Fred Dawson usually accompanied me and one Thursday, I had my lunch and called for him at his house, to go back for afternoon school. His parents were getting ready to go to St. Neots market and Fred, who did not like school all that much, tried to persuade his parents to let him go with them. I could see that it was going to be a battle of wills and there was only going to be one winner, when Mr. Dawson reached up to the main beam, running along the ceiling and brought down a horse whip, which had obviously been used as a persuader before and quite quickly Fred was running down the lane, with Mr. Dawson in hot pursuit, cracking the whip around Fred's ankles. I doubt if Fred played him up again after that little episode and I do not think it would have done some of today's youngsters any harm to have a taste of that medicine.

I really cannot see how one can discipline those who are badly behaved and unruly, without some form of corporal punishment. No one likes pain, which is why none of us likes going to the dentist and it is the fear of pain, or consequences that stops wrongdoing. Unless parents and teachers are allowed to administer an early slap on the backside, we shall all be the worse for it. Our Dad used to have a thick leather belt and he was not afraid to give us one, when it was necessary and although it was not nice at the time, I think it hurt ones pride more than the flesh, but it probably had the desired effect, to teach us to behave properly.

9

In the infants' class, we were expected to learn the 2, 3 and 4 times tables and chanting them in unison in a singsong voice, was a useful way of remembering them. The thick curtain separating the two rooms did not keep out the sounds from next door and most of us knew the 5, 6 and 7 times tables before we went into the 'big room'. I am sure everyone is the same, in that every building seemed immense then, when we were children and Pertenhall School was no exception, but now when I go there for a function, it seems to get smaller, almost too small to hold the memories of those early days.

Another popular playground activity was spinning tops, especially in the springtime – why then? I have no idea! Of course there were races from one end of the playground to the other, which ended with the first one home to touch the fence, next to old Mr. Day's property. Why I remember this incident so clearly, was because all of us finished together, in what is now known as a blanket finish, about six of us in a line, which was too much for the fence, which had had enough of boys crashing into it for so many years and the wood, no doubt, getting more rotten every year. The fence broke off level with the ground and we all finished in a heap on top of it. Luckily, none of us was hurt and surprise, surprise, none of us got into trouble over it and someone presumably got paid by someone to put it back up again.

Around about this time, a tragic accident occurred, which resulted in a very popular man losing his life. The man was Mr. Abraham, the father of Gordon and the family where our sister Fay was fostered out to when our mother died. Mr. Abraham played in the Kimbolton

Brass Band and one evening in August, he was coming home on his motor bike, round The Avenue where the road narrowed at the bridge, unawares that a farmer was bringing his binder home, without a rear light on the vehicle and in the dusk, Mr. Abraham did not see or hear the vehicle and crashed his motorbike into it. He was fatally injured and died in hospital shortly afterwards. The family moved away soon after this, which meant the end of the little sweet shop that Mrs. Abrahams used to run. This meant that the village of Pertenhall had no shop, no pub, no electricity, and no mains water. It had a church, and an old vicar named the Reverend Mosely, a Moravian Chapel with a minister, a post office, run by Mrs. Hardwicke and the Chadwell Spring, that emerged out of the ground, about 300 yards upstream of the brook behind Chadwell Holding Cottage and about 30 yards on the south side of the brook.

My Grandmother told me that when she was a girl, an underground pipe, parallel to the brook, brought the water from the spring to Chadwell Lane and a pewter cup on a chain, secured to a wooden post enabled travellers to help themselves to a drink of the excellent water. The underground pipe was cut through, by the person who farmed the holding, sometime in the early 1930's and the supply to the cup was terminated. Soon after the cup went missing and with it a village amenity which could be returned if enough enthusiastic inhabitants were to stir themselves and do something that would provide a landmark and a memorial of good things of the past.

★

Another feature missing from the landscape is the large number, probably 100 or more, of the magnificent elm trees, which lined either side of the B660 from the weigh post, which is where the Lt.Staughton Road turns left, just below the bottom of Chapel Hill, through the village to the crossroads at Green End and also the road leading out of the village, in the direction of Swineshead. Many of these Elms were growing in the fields that were permanent pasture and with all being about the same size, would point to a planting project being carried out and if this was the case, a very successful one too. That all these Elms succumbed to the Dutch Elm disease and disappeared in the late 1960's-early 1970's was a great shame, especially to those of us who came to look upon them as making Pertenhall something special.

Another feature of the village was the number of allotments, between 25 and 30, which started at the top of Chapel Hill and went down on the left hand side, to the weigh post. Again, more allotments, up the right hand side of the road, below where the council houses are, up the Bedford Road, following on towards the Green End crossroads, towards the ditch that goes down March Field.

There used to be a pub down Wood End Lane, named the 'Bugle Horn'. This burnt down in somewhat mysterious circumstances. The brewery held the license, but this was purchased by a rich old lady called Miss Pope, who lived in the big house at the top of Chapel Hill. Miss Pope wanted to ensure that no pub could be built in the village after that. She did not agree with men going to the pub to spend all their wages, leaving their families short of money and so she found a way of making sure that did not happen.

Soon after the fatherless Abraham family moved out of the village, their house became occupied by a large family named McClelland. They had a number of children and the eldest daughter, Lucy, was the same age as my sister Stancy and one Saturday, when these two girls were about 12 years of age, Stancy had gone round there to play. Lucy, however, had been left to get the lunch for her four or five younger sisters and brothers, as their parents had gone shopping to Bedford. Lucy decided to make them Yorkshire pudding, but as she was unable to find an egg in the house, decided to put custard powder into the mixture instead. I doubt whether this was a success, but Lucy was a very resourceful girl, as was borne out, when a year or so later, all the schoolchildren went to the seaside by coach. Not only did it rain all day, but it was bitterly cold into the bargain. Lucy's younger brothers and sisters were in thin summer clothes and were in danger of catching pneumonia. Lucy went to a newsagents shop and asked if they had any old newspapers. The shopkeeper must have been a decent kind of chap because between them, they wrapped up these four little kids in newspapers and tied them up like parcels, just leaving their arms, legs and heads sticking out and that is how they still were when we got back to Pertenhall later that evening. Robert was several years younger than Lucy and passed his entrance exam to Kimbolton School in 1937.

*

I probably went up to the 'Big Room' in the school in 1932 and the teacher was Miss Mason, a farmer's daughter from High Park Farm, between Stonely and Easton. She travelled to school by bicycle, except one winter, when a heavy fall of snow made the roads impassable by bicycle, but Miss Mason, undaunted, came on one of her father's horses and stabled it next door with Mr. Day. The journey must have been a good three and a half miles each way, so she certainly earned her money, just by coming and going, with two steep hills to traverse in each direction, let alone teaching all day.

Miss Mason was very strict and there was no slacking allowed. As well as normal subjects, Miss Mason taught us how to make baskets and how to make peg rugs, which were made with any old bits of cloth we could find. We also learned country dancing and Miss Mason made our lessons very interesting and she taught to the level of the pupil's ability, which stood everyone in good stead for the life ahead.

I was lucky to get away lightly with a prank that went wrong. Coming up to Guy Fawkes night, we were in the playground at afternoon break, and I had a 'Little Demon' firework in my pocket and one of the other boys had found an old and empty 'Vim' tin that the school cleaner had discarded. I stuck the Little Demon in one of the holes in the top of the empty tube and lit the blue touch paper. When it went off, the force of the explosion lifted off the metal lid, which shot up about 20 feet and landed on top of the school roof. It then proceeded to come jinking down the tiles and land outside the door, just as Miss Mason came rushing out to see what was going on. That she should select me as the culprit was absolutely spot on and I have never failed to be amazed that the school masters and mistresses have been so accurate in their assumptions. I suppose it is what is known as intuition. The punishment for me was to stand in the corner, facing the wall. I considered that I got away lightly.

Another prank I was pleased not to be involved in happened at Swineshead School just before it closed, and the mistress was called Miss Yeo. Like at Pertenhall School, in those days, amenities were scarce, and toilets were the bucket type, with a door at the back for the handyman to take the bucket out for emptying, from time to time. Some of the older boys worked out that Miss Yeo went to the girls' toilet during the afternoon break. One of the boys crept round the back and hid by the back door of the toilet, whilst another boy gave him the signal when she went in the front door. Just as the teacher sat on the seat, the boy opened the back door and had a gloved hand, clutching a large bunch of stinging nettles, which he administered to Miss Yeo's unprotected bum. He quickly shut the door and went back round the front and carried on playing, as if nothing had happened.

I have often wondered what part of her anatomy was the most coloured, her face or her bottom. The boy that did that dastardly deed joined the navy in 1938 and served throughout the war, unscathed, including being on board a cruiser during the Salerno landings in Italy, which took a direct hit from a bomb, which went straight down the funnel, into the engine room and killed everyone in that room. What a waste of manhood is war and is any country any better off when the war has ended?

There is a Reason for Everything

I started at Pertenhall School on the day after my fourth birthday. I was taken there by Grandma in the buggy (small horse and cart). It was a Church of England School and the vicar, Reverend Mosely, came on the first morning of each school term, to say prayers and sing a hymn, before lessons began. He was a creepy old character and never really mixed with any of the villagers.

His living was provided for by the rent from two farms, Grange Farm, run by the Shelton family and Hall Farm, run by the Stewarts. Later on, Sam Stuart and his son Bernie, went to farm at Bromham, leaving younger son, Herbie, to carry on farming at Pertenhall. Now Bernie's grandsons still farm the land at Pertenhall, growing continuous wheat, which seems to perform quite well, although with today's price of £100 per ton, can only be about break even.

Grandma, as I have written before, was a very religious person and attended both morning and evening services at the Church on Sundays.

She once quoted me a rhyme about the reason for some of the congregations' attendances at church, which went something like this: –

Some go there to see and be seen.
Others go to say they have been.

Some go there to meet a lover.
Others go there to see another.

Some go there to laugh and talk.
Others go there just for the walk.

Some go there to doze and nod.
But few go there to worship God.

I recently attended Edna Nicholson's funeral at Swineshead Church, which was packed with mourners. Edna was in my first class at Pertenhall School and was in the school photo in *Once a Man – Twice a Boy.* Edna had more recently been enjoying the company of others in an old folks' home in Raunds and it was always a pleasure to visit her and talk over old times. As Edna's health deteriorated, the inevitable came to pass. She will be sadly missed by family and friends, but we may meet again, if as the scriptures say, in the life hereafter.

CHAPTER TWO

Changes in Agriculture in Pertenhall from 1930 – 2005

My Grandparents

Grandfather Banks was always known as Harry (even though his names were Henry Charles) and his friends called him, "Harry Boy". He was a big man by any standards, six and half feet tall and weighing at his peak 22 stone. He was a hard businessman and an extremely able farmer and did not suffer fools gladly, or even at all! Grandma Banks, formerly Kate Reynolds, before she married grandfather, was just about the complete opposite. A tiny person of not much more than five feet tall and slim with it. She was kindness personified, not only to her family, but anyone in the village who was poorly or down on their luck. Grandma would visit with a basket full of goodies, some eggs, a freshly baked cake and some fruit from the orchard. She walked to church twice on a Sunday and read a passage from the bible every night before retiring to bed. The marriage was blessed with three children, Harry, who married Grace Stanton and had three boys, Henry, Victor and Kendrick, Amy the only daughter who did not marry, as apparently her boyfriend had been killed in the first world war and she was content to be a maiden Aunt and finally, Charles William, my father, who married Lily Noble.

Dad was the youngest, being born on 3rd June 1900. About a week after Dad was born, a violent thunderstorm hit the village and the church was struck by lightning and around 20 foot of the steeple was sent crashing to the ground.

Another even worse disaster to strike the village had happened in 1905, when, after a suffocating hot afternoon, a massive thunderstorm approached from the SW and, amidst thunder and lightening, a shattering hailstorm swept a mile wide swathe through the village, with hailstones as big as golf balls smashing all the windows on the south-west facing side of houses and devastating the ripening corn that was just ready for the binder. The disaster was so bad that a fund was set up by the local newspaper, to help those hardest hit, otherwise farmers and small-holders would have gone out of business.

Grandfather moved to Manor Farm, Pertenhall around 1918 and Uncle Harry carried on farming at Hill Farm in Lt.Staughton. Dad married in 1920 and Stancy was born in the little white cottage at the bottom of Spring Hill on 2nd February 1921. They moved to Chadwell Farm, Pertenhall a couple of years later. I was born on 25th January 1926, during the time of the General Strike and this meant that all government offices were closed for several weeks. When Dad, together with one of his friends, driving the pony and trap, went to register my birth, the fact that they got the day I was born wrong by only two days, having called in at too many pubs along the way (according to Granny Banks), was no mean feat, although it has done me out of two days of my old age pension!

Manor Farm at Pertenhall was 660 acres and Grandfather rented, in addition to this, quite a lot of available ridge and furrow grassland, at Stonely, which was rented from Pembroke College at Cambridge and this land was only accessed via Hatchet Lane. The land, known as "The Colleges ", was used to graze his large flocks of sheep and cattle, which allowed the home pastures to rest. I used to journey frequently with one of the stockmen, by horse and cart from Pertenhall to Stonely, to shepherd and feed these sheep, according to the time of the year.

There was a massive range of outbuildings that went with the farm at Pertenhall, which housed livestock and the provisions to feed them. Two of the largest barns were filled with sheaves of corn and quite a number of corn stacks were made, out in the "rick yard". There were two large yards for cattle aged between 1-2 years and one yard for milking cows. There was another yard for young stock, a pig yard and a host of calf pens and pig sties, with a lambing yard as well. Plenty of straw was needed for litter during the winter. The older bullocks that would be fattened the following summer, would winter out in sheltered pastures and were fed hay and mangolds as required. These buildings were like an Aladdin's cave to young inquisitive boys, and we were encouraged to help whenever possible, and this is where the seeds of future farmers are grown.

On modern farms nowadays, things are so very different, with huge combine harvesters and grain trailers, driers and the like, all of which make farms dangerous places, not like in the 1930's when horsepower was king, and life went along at an orderly pace.

Early Years

Life in Pertenhall in the early years of the 1930's saw us with no electricity or mains water and public transport consisted of one bus per week to Bedford and back on a Saturday. There was a church with a vicar and the Moravian Chapel with a minister. The village consisted of around 60 houses, occupied by about 70 women, 60 or so men and just over 40 children, the latter who attended the Church of England and Risely schools. All of the men, (except one who went to work at the Igranic works in Bedford), worked on the local farms, or as gardeners and roadmen. There were about 17 farms or small holdings, ranging from the largest farm at 800 acres, to the smallest farm of about 8-10 acres. Some of the small holders had part-time jobs on the larger farms, but basically their main living was from the holding. Probably three quarters of all the land was rented, with the main owners being the Colleges at Oxford and Cambridge and the Church Commissioners.

Horsepower and manpower were the main motive forces, with steam power in the form of steam engines, which drove the portable thrashing tackle and steam cultivating engines that were owned by contractors who moved from farm to farm, according to seasonal requirements.

The first tractors appeared about 1934-35 and were made by Fordson, powered by internal combustion engines, and ran on paraffin. However, they required a

*Gathering the stooks. Everyone mucking in –Miss Modlen on the left,
who lived in a cottage near Manor Farm and Bob Roddis in uniform.*

small amount of petrol for starting the engine, which was
done with a crank handle and on frosty mornings this was
not a job to volunteer for, as a backfire would send the
unwary operator into orbit or leave him with a sprained
wrist at the very least and increased the range of vocabulary
of small boys who were watching the operation from a safe
distance!

The small holdings were mainly pasture, with cattle
and poultry the sources of income. A yardstick for 'stocking
rates' suggested that one acre of good grazing land would
support one milking cow or two followers or 10 sheep.
Some pasture had to be set-a-side for haymaking, which
was probably the most nerve-wracking time of the farming
year. Good quality hay was one of the most treasured

commodities, as catchy weather at the vital time could prove disastrous. The best farmers had a stack or so of good hay in reserve. A well thatched stack would keep good for three or four years.

There is probably not an exact acreage which distinguishes a farm from a small holding, but my definition is that a man was presumed to be a farmer if he had enough land to keep himself employed throughout the year and then employed other labourers when required.

My grandfather farmed approximately 800 acres and employed about 15 regular men, with casual labour brought in at busy times, such as hay time, harvest and shearing, to take up the slack. It was traditional that shearing would be operational by the first Wednesday in June, and that was the day "The Derby" was run. Most of the gang of men would have three-pence each way on one of the runners. When I was a small boy, I used to go around the farm with grandfather in his pony and cart, to check on the progress of the work. My job was to jump down and open and shut the gates. With the farm being about 50 % arable and 50 % pasture, there were plenty of gates that needed negotiating.

I have never ceased to be amazed at the skill required by farmers from that era to be successful with the limited number of resources at their disposal and it would take a whole library, not just a book to describe in detail the intricacies of the farming system in those bygone days. Farming was not learned from a book, or at agricultural college; no officials from the Ministry of Agriculture or D.E.F.R.A. were available at the end of a telephone, because in those days they did not exist. The knowledge came, I imagine, from the hereditary genes, passed on from one generation to the next. Most of the best farmers today come from a long line of farming stock; similarly with the best racehorses, where their bloodlines can be traced back countless generations. These are recorded in the stud books, but with homo sapiens, no such book is available, not to my knowledge anyway. We all know who our mothers are, but there is not so much certainty over the other half of our parentage. Experience is the other commodity that is needed in any business, not just farming and is one of the few things that money cannot buy. There are plenty of "I told you so" merchants around, but not too many who can foresee the problems before they arise. It is not so much those who do the most things right who are successful, but those who do the least things wrong!

One of the fundamental requirements of farming is to keep the fertility of the soil stable and in bygone days, before artificial fertilizers became available, the soil had to be kept in good heart by farmyard manure, which is a bi-product of livestock keeping. The cattle would be over-wintered in yards that were littered daily with straw. Hay would be provided and "short grub" – the technical term for ground mangle-wurzels and crushed oats and beans or peas, mixed with chaff, fed into the mangers in the mornings. The manure would be hand forked out onto carts in the spring and would then be put into a clamp called a muckle, which was allowed to heat up and rot down and was then spread over selected fields after harvest. This was very time consuming and the fields closest to the farm buildings were the ones that usually got the muck cart. The fields further away had a turn in the rotation of a root crop of turnips or swedes. This was what

Threshing machine. Note the sacks from Banks' Sandy – the corn merchants.

the sheep were folded on to provide the fertility. The sheep were known as 'the golden hoof' and a well-managed flock were a good source of income. An expert knowledge was needed, because vets' bills were unwelcomed and a top-quality shepherd was a prized asset. The folding was done by moveable wooden partitions called hurdles and were made from ash, taken from the farm spinneys. They were cut down when about four to five years old and would be as thick as a man's wrist. These would be left to dry for a month or so and every springtime, an old guy used to turn up for two or three days, sleeping rough in one of the farm buildings at night and turned this heap of ash poles into a neat pile of hurdles, which, if handled properly, would last for up to 10 years. These fields of root crops for folding would be bordered on at least one side by a grass field for the sheep to run back onto at night and if the weather had turned nasty. Hay racks were provided as a back up and were a good barometer for when the fold needed extending.

Those were the days when, not only artificial fertiliser was unavailable, but chemical sprays for control of weeds and disease had not been invented. So, it was by the timing of the cultivations and clever rotation of the crops that sorted out the men from the boys! Autumn drilled crops out-yielded spring sown ones, but to drill too early meant that the weeds, like blackgrass and wild oats got a flying start. They would smother the crop and drain the soil of its precious nutrients. Winter sowing would be delayed on most fields until after the beginning of November. Winter wheat would probably be the most profitable crop but would only be grown twice during a six-year rotation. These rotations were quite flexible, but, by and large, wheat was only followed by a summer fallow or a crop of clover, or beans, peas or tares, which are legumes and have the power to leave a supply of nitrogen behind in the soil. A typical rotation might look something like this:-

1. Summer fallow
2. Winter wheat
3. Spring barley (under-sown with clover or a mixture of clover and rye grass)
4. Clover or grass crop for hay
5. Winter wheat
6. Winter or spring oats
7. Beans peas or tares
8. Winter wheat and then the cycle would go round again

A typical yield of grain in those days would be between a ton and 25cwt (hundred-weight). The wheat would be sold to a merchant and had to be transported to Kimbolton

Railway Station. The wheat was sold in sacks of 18 stone, Oats 12 stone, Barley 16 stone and Beans, Peas and Tares 20 stone.

A horse and cart would carry about one ton – about eight or nine sacks. A wagon, pulled by two horses in shafts could carry two ton. An extra two horses were to accompany this cavalcade, one to pitch onto the front of each cart or wagon in turn, to pull the load, first of all up Chapel Hill in Pertenhall and then as soon as the first cart was at the top of the hill, this went on and was pulled up Buskett Hill in the same way and then onto the station to be unloaded. The spare horse would be taken back down the hill to help pull up the second cart or wagon and so on until all had arrived at the station and been emptied. This job was often undertaken on a Saturday morning, and everyone had to look lively, or they would be late home for knocking off time (half day Saturday).

The men worked about 44 hours per week, five and a half eight hour days, but in what was called the harvest month, the hours were 6am until 8pm with time out for meal breaks.

Before the War

The top man, namely the horse-keeper always turned up for work one hour before anyone else, to give the working horses a good meal before they started work. When the horses were doing the really heavy stuff such as ploughing, two o'clock was their limit, a six-hour day for them. Several of the senior workmen lived in tied cottages, which were virtually rent free with a couple of hours work feeding the animals on a Sunday morning squaring it all up. The horse-keeper earned 30 shillings a week, which was one pound ten shillings or £1.50 in today's money and a sliding scale down to a 14-year-old boy who would start on ten shillings or 50p per week. To compare the costs with today, 30 shillings would buy the following – 30 packets of 20 Players Cigarettes or 45 packets of 20 Woodbines, (which nearly all the men smoked). Or 24 gallons of petrol, but that was pretty irrelevant, because only four people in Pertenhall had a car! Or 120 helpings of Fish and Chips. Wrens van from St. Neots toured around the villages on a Thursday evening, calling at Pertenhall Wood End and Green End. In the summer, Thursday evening was when the cricket team had their practice night and finished up with a piece of fish for 2d (pence) and a helping of chips for a penny and that was a good meal.

Most of the big farms in those days brewed their own beer and at harvest, hay time, shearing and threshing, the men were given several pints of free beer. This was a good quality, energy providing supplement for the men when work was hard and arduous.

I have painted a picture of idyllic rural life, but I was to learn, as the years passed, that everything in the garden was not as it appeared. The trouble had started in 1921, which was the driest year anyone before, or since had experienced. There was virtually no harvest of spring sown crops, as the seed never germinated on the lighter soils. The pastures were bare by mid-July and to keep the stock alive, branches from trees and hedges were cut down to provide feed for the animals. Water had to be transported long distances, as wells had dried up. On Grandfather's farm, they did not have that problem, because when the farmstead was built, a spring up on the high ground, about half a mile away, had been piped to a header tank straight into the house and all the farm buildings. Also, the Chadwell Spring kept running and was a source of water for the rest of the village and beyond.

Quickly on the heels of the drought, came the worldwide financial crash, where the value of produce and wages were cut by 50 % overnight. Very soon, those who were the most vulnerable went to the wall, but established businesses had a bit of fat to fall back on, as there had been a few good years following the end of the 1914-1918 war. Back then, people saved up for rainy days, but it was not to last, and as the years ticked by, the situation became markedly worse for everyone. Business was dire, with the cost of producing a ton of wheat far greater than it would realise when sold. Large families were the norm in those days, whether by accident or design, the babies kept turning up and another mouth to feed for already stretched family finances. Some people turned to drink for solace, but that only made the problem worse. Nervous breakdowns were commonplace and often lead to the inevitable. Many children were left with only one parent, but families in those days were close knit and closed ranks around the unfortunate. Ageing grandparents were not dumped in the nearest old folks' home but were found a niche in the family home where they could retain their dignity and the illegitimate children, of which there were quite a number, were given love within the family circle.

The problem in the farming industry was the amount of food imported from overseas, often produced by cheap labour. Successive governments, keen to get re-elected, were happy to see cheap food for the masses and not a thought for what might happen, if and when the umbilical cord was cut.

The first shaft of light emerging from the dark tunnel came around 1935, when a big dairy was opened at Fenstanton. A lorry would come round the villages daily, collecting the milk. Prior to this, the milk had the cream separated from it and made into butter, which was sold with the eggs and other produce at the local markets. Seven or eight farmers in Pertenhall quickly turned to this new form of milk production and the monthly cheque from the dairy at least meant that they had a little money in their pockets, and it certainly kept the wolf from the door, for those who had cows in milk at the time.

As the 1930's meandered on, more and more land became overgrown with bushes and trees. Nature is not slow in reclaiming derelict land, as the birds feeding on the seeds of blackberry, hawthorn, and blackthorn etc spread the seeds far and wide, after their bodies had digested the fleshy part of the fruit and although it is hypothetical, but had the second world war not happened, I am sure that this part of the country would resemble Sherwood Forest in Robin Hood's time by now! My grandfather gave up the unequal struggle in the autumn of 1937, having farmed continuously for 50 years (apparently without ever taking a holiday). He was desperately unlucky not to be able to enjoy a few years of comfortable retirement as a reward for this lifetime of hard work. He died three weeks after his farm sale, following an operation to alleviate prostate gland problems, which sadly went very wrong. He died in a nursing home in De Parys Avenue in Bedford.

The Haywain, a wonderful sight.

A little postscript to this story. Following the death of Claude's grandfather, his grandmother, Kate Banks, to whom Dad was absolutely devoted, moved to live in a cottage in the High Street in Kimbolton, with her daughter, Claude's Aunt Amy. Kate sadly died in the summer of 1944. Dad told me that he was so distraught at her death, when he was 18 years old, that he was unable to attend her funeral because he could not trust himself not to cry in front of everyone and that would not be the done thing.

The War Years

By 1938, the political climate had begun to change. Germany under Hitler had started to flex its muscles and rearm and rebuild faster than the terms of agreement from its surrender in 1918. The League of Nations, which was an early edition of the United Nations and equally inefficient, did nothing to stop Germany from gobbling up its weaker neighbours. However, when it invaded Poland in September 1939, England and France had had enough, and war was declared at 11am on Sunday 3rd September 1939. With only 20 years separating the two world conflicts and the havoc caused by the few submarines that Germany had towards the end of 1918, our politicians were mighty slow in realising that a wolf might be creeping up to our door. Politicians seem to be very good at talking but are afraid of taking drastic action because too few of them have the experience of running a business and having to grasp the mettle and make decisions on the hoof. Back then, as now, politicians, when in trouble order an enquiry, which takes the form of a committee to tackle the problem. One of the problems in 1939 was that we had been importing too much cheap food from abroad, whilst many of our farmers had gone broke and the land had become overgrown and derelict.

The committee elected to sort out the almighty mess we now found ourselves in was named The War Agricultural Executive Committee (or War Ag for short!) Farming implements and tractors were purchased, and labour was engaged to farm the land which had become derelict. Various grants became available, the first one being £2 per acre for farmers who were willing to plough up pasture fields for growing crops. This did not go down too well with most farmers, as this meant more work and at that time, no guarantee of any increase in income. However, with the U-boats becoming effective, the light began to dawn on the powers that be that we may be in trouble with the food supply. The ploughing up policy now became compulsory and any farmer who did not comply had his land confiscated and it would be farmed by the newly formed "War Ag." Prices were raised and set at a control level and more tractors were seen around, as funds to buy them became available. Artificial fertilisers now entered the market and one of the biggest boons for increased crop yield was a new drill, imported from North America, known as the combine drill, which had two hoppers, one for seed and the other for artificial fertiliser. We got one of these for drilling in the autumn of 1941 and using phosphate with the seed, the results were quite significantly increased yields and with the perfect weather conditions for harvesting from 1939-1945, probably saved the country.

At last, with some money in the bank, the farmers were able to buy this new machinery, but more labour was needed and some of the young men had been called up into the services. So those still too young to go to war and those too old filled the gaps and as the war progressed, the food rations were cut, and life began to resemble a dog chasing its tail! It is quite amazing how morale kept as high as it did, when news of battles being lost, and ships sunk was the norm and the sound of German planes overhead nearly every night became as regular as putting the cat out! I think it was listening to Churchill's speeches on the radio that did the trick – what a man! It is a pity that some of today's politicians were not around in 1939-1945, as they would know the way to behave and an old saying that "Honest men are few and far between", rings particularly true. "Lies, damned lies and politicians," also springs to mind!

A welcome addition to our labour force were the Prisoners of War (POW's). We had Italians and very good workers they were too. We had two billeted in one of our farm cottages and they were as good as any of the local men, especially when they learned the language and the lay-out of the farm. When they were repatriated in 1945, we had land girls for a time. This was quite nice for us young chaps, but Dad reckoned that we would get more work done if they were not around, and he was probably right!

The first combine harvesters that appeared were owned by the War Ag., but with the extra labour and fine weather, we on our farm could cope quite well. Long hours had to be put in but sitting on a tractor was not too bad, compared to walking along all day beside a horse. Lorries were available to collect the harvested grain and as the war news gradually improved, and the sight of the American B17's taking off from the host of local airdromes to deliver to Germany a taste of what they had given us, was a welcome relief from spending so much time on the proverbial ropes. These massive planes looked so formidable as they circled to gain height and create the box formation required to be effective against the enemy fighters. But, by late afternoon and depending on how far into occupied Europe they had to penetrate to reach their target, they limped back home in a sorry state. In singles and in pairs, with engines stopped, holes punched through their wings and fuselages and young men, in many cases only 18 or 19 years old and probably shot to bits in their metal coffins. The nadir was the day they were sent to Swinefort to bomb the ball-bearing factory, across the far side of Germany. One third of the total force of 180 B17's did not come back and the American 8th Airforce group at Kimbolton saw one of the highest losses. Brave blokes they were, and I take my hat off to them.

Bob Roddis, a proud member of the Pertenhall Home Guard

The 1950's

Mercifully, the war ended in 1945 and the country began to recover, although rationing went on into the 1950's. Life on the farm meant adapting to more modern times. Following the wonderful summers of the war years, we came right back down to earth with the nightmare harvest of 1946, when many crops were lost altogether. This was followed by the frost and snow in early 1947, where the roads were blocked for several days by 15 feet snow drifts and the milk lorry could not get through to collect the milk. We had milk stored in every conceivable container, including the family bath!

Modern machinery was gradually replacing labour and anyway, as wages were higher in the local towns and factories, the drift away from the land was soon gathering pace. As the farm incomes increased, so the expenses went up with them. Owner occupiers had their farmhouses and tied cottages to bring up to more modern standards. Electricity, which had come to Pertenhall across the fields from Stonely in 1935, when Victor Cunnard of the White Shipping Line bought the Old Rectory in the village and was the first house to get the supply connected. No one else could afford to have electricity connected until after the war, so this then became another expense on top of repairs and installing modern sanitation, all of which is taken for granted today. A bath in front of the fire once a month and the toilet at the bottom of the garden was either a good thing or a bad one, according to which way you looked at it, but it did not seem to have done much harm to yours truly! Dad brought our first combine harvester, a 10-foot tractor drawn "Minneapolis Moline", which cost £880 and no prizes for guessing where it came from. Today new combines are up to 30-foot, self-propelled and cost £250,000.

The flash flood on 20th May 1950, when five inches of rain fell in an hour on a Sunday afternoon and a ten-year-old girl was swept to her death by rising flood water in the village of Pertenhall, has left a lasting impression in the minds of those who were around to witness that tragic event. The powers of nature have no bounds and man is helpless in certain circumstances and sometimes all we can do is pray to ease our troubled minds.

The wet harvests of 1952, 1954 and 1955 alerted farmers to the fact that combine harvesters were not the be all and end all of farming problems, because a barn full of wet grain was a bigger headache than no harvest at all. Grain driers of various sizes and variety were soon available, but this meant more expense and as one farmer pointed out – "Something else to go wrong!" But driers became a must, none-the-less, and like bicycles and then the motor car, soon every farmer had one!

As the 1940's went into the 1950's, most of the local farmers who had had to resort to milking cows to balance the budget, reverted back to what they were best at, that is mixed farming, leaning more towards the arable. The milking side was taken up by Scottish farmers moving south and soon the pastures were occupied by the Red and White Ayrshire cows, soon to be replaced by the more prolific milkers, the Black and White Friesians.

Our father, Charles William Banks was very unlucky with his health and passed away just before his 60th birthday in 1959. However, he had given brother Bob and me a good grounding in farming and life in general. He had a house built on our land at Stonely for Daphne and me when we were married in 1955. Bob also married Gwen in 1955 and they lived in a cottage adjacent to Chadwell Farm, where we were all born. There was not a lot of money to play with when Bob and I took over the farm, which was none too big to support two families, so we decided to sell all of our livestock, which had been our father's pride and joy and to plough up the grassland, buy some decent machinery with the proceeds of the sale of the livestock and get down to the serious business of earning enough money to keep our families, which over the first few years, rapidly increased in size. Luck was on our side in the decisions we made and with hard work and burning the candle at both ends, we were able to achieve our goal. Perhaps we have not been as financially successful as many of our contemporaries, but money only comes second to happiness, although good health comes before either of them and one is often dependent on the other.

A Farmers eye view of the Winter of 1962-63

The winter of 1962-63 was not as severe, nor lasted as long as the winter of 1946-47. However, one of the factors that made it so memorable and so difficult to live through, was the lack of a good depth of snow, which would have kept the frost from penetrating the ground, deeper than the water pipes, that serviced many of the homes in this area. All the families who were affected will never forget having to cope with a nightmare scenario and each will have their own story to tell.

Daphne and myself, along with our three children aged six years old, four years old and 21 months old, lived at College Farm, Hatchet Lane, Stonely and we were without mains water for between a month and six weeks. Quite how we managed is difficult to comprehend, especially looking back from what is now more than a 50-year vantage point, but being up a creek without a canoe, let alone a paddle, is about as near as I can get to it! Nowadays, if the water is off for a couple of days, people are jumping up and down like Zulu chiefs and threatening to sue the water authority!

We quickly organised our lives into a damage limitation programme. As soon as Daphne had the breakfast cleared away and the eldest daughter off to school, she collected snow to melt in large preserving pans on the Aga, which supplied the day's water to flush the toilet in the bathroom. The outside toilet had frozen up in sympathy with the water pipes. We contacted half a dozen of our friends and relatives and arranged to visit them, on a rota basis, for us all to bath at regular intervals. At sometime during each day, I would go up to Chadwell Farm, Pertenhall, where my brother Bob, who was a partner in our farming business, lived with his family. I would fill an old ten-gallon milk churn with water for all the family laundry, cooking and drinking requirements, which the melted snow had not catered for.

Although the Aga normally heated the water, the plumbing system was such that if we drew off hot water, we would have had to carry the cold water up into the header tank in the loft, which was obviously a non-starter. So, all the kettles and saucepans, instead of sitting around and calling one another black, were on the Aga, providing what we all take for granted nowadays, a constant supply of hot water.

The other downside of the frost and snow was the fact that one of our farm's cash crops at that time was Brussels sprouts, which needed to be picked frost-free. However, for at least a month, if not longer, it froze both day and night.

The local wood pigeon population did not seem to mind if the Brussels were frozen, or not and just descended on the sprouts in their thousands, with no other food available for them at the time of year. A pigeon is like a rat, in that it will eat almost anything when times are hard. They had exhausted all the autumn fruits and berries, acorns, sloes, hips and hawes and ivy berries, and with clover and chickweed covered with snow, it was eat sprouts or die! As the cold got stronger, they had to eat more and more to stay alive. The physical energy used up in flying is far more than running and frozen brassicas are probably one of the poorest suppliers of energy. Each evening the pigeons struggled back to the woods to roost and to escape the icy blast for a few hours, with their crops so full and prominent, they reminded me of overendowed waitresses!

At first light, the birds were heading back to the sprout fields, where the farmers and their friends were laying in wait to defend the crop, which they hoped, when the thaw eventually came, would fetch a good price in the markets.

Pigeons, like most birds, have to drink and with all the ponds and brooks frozen solid, any running water was like a magnet and Chadwell Springs resembled just that. Cartridges (for guns) in the end were in such short supply and as the birds were worthless because they were so thin, the economics raised the standard of shooting to a high degree!

The Thaw, when it eventually came, was a blessed relief and ended an experience I would not like to live through again, but adversity brings communities closer together and without some bad times, we are not likely to appreciate the good ones.

The story unfortunately did not have a happy ending, as far as the sprout crop was concerned. A week after the thaw, the sprout crop collapsed into a stinking rotten morass and the carcasses of literally thousands of pigeons littered the sprout fields. It was more like a scene from Dante's Inferno than England's Green and Pleasant Land.

The family of five lived to tell the tale and as for the pigeons, they have had to learn to live on oilseed rape.

Penny's memories of the winter of 1962-63

Reading Dad's story has been particularly poignant to me, as I remember the time very well and also because the story of the winter of 1962-63 has featured in a recent series of the popular television programme, 'Call the Midwife'.

I do not recall us not having milk delivered during this period, as depicted in the television programme, although this might be because we still had a small dairy herd and could provide for our own needs. I do recollect Dad telling me about the winter of 1947, where dairy farmers struggled to get the milk off the farms, as the roads were impassable. I am certain there were milk shortages then and quite possibly for town folk in '62-'63.

I was the six-year-old in Dad's story and can transport myself back to this incredibly cold winter, full of admiration for my parents in the struggle they had, for probably two months, especially when you consider, that now a days, the whole country seems to grind to a halt after just a dusting of snow.

I remember my father coming in with the washing up bowl heaped high with fresh frozen snow to tip into the huge saucepan, which was permanently on the go on the AGA to provide water for washing up, washing and flushing the toilets. As this cold spell seemed to go on forever, he had to go further and further each day to collect this precious commodity of snow for our most basic needs.

I vividly remember being taken to various homes of friends of our parents and relatives for our weekly bath.

Auntie Audrey Bates at Wornditch Farm was probably our most frequent destination. Uncle Burt and Auntie Audrey did not have children of their own, so were always pleased to see us and I am sure we caused less disruption to them. Whereas our other visits to the Sheltons at Pertenhall and Dad's brother and wife, Uncle Bob and Auntie Gwen, also at Pertenhall and Tommy and Audrey Newman at Gt. Staughton, all had their own small children to contend with, without someone else's three small children landing on them for baths and hair wash!

I remember that eventually the thaw came and for quite some time, it seemed strange seeing grass again and the roads and everything getting back to normal as we escaped from what had seemed, for so long, like an arctic wilderness.

The Best Years for Farming

Around 1982 Bob and I decided to dissolve the partnership, as his son Brian had joined the business and they had their own ideas of how they wanted to run their farm at Pertenhall and I would farm down at Stonely. I think the 1980's was probably the best decade for farming, as far as I can recollect, whilst others might say the 1970's or the 1990's and I would not argue.

What is more certain is the fact that the present government would be more than happy if there were no farmers in this country. With cheap imports flooding in, we are back to the 1930's mentality. "You don't miss the water until the well runs dry", is an old saying that comes to mind at this time. Like farming, everything is cyclical if you wait long enough.

Wheat yields are now up to four tons per acre and any farm with less than 500 acres will struggle to provide a living for a father and son. We are back to the dog chasing its tail again, with so many rules and regulations to comply with and forms to fill in, detailing every product used in the growing of crops or the rearing of livestock. What I know sticks in the craw of the farming community is the plain fact that imported grain from eastern Europe is coming in and unloaded at our ports with absolutely no knowledge of how it was produced, stored and transported.

Meat is coming in from countries who have endemic diseases like foot and mouth, and which was proved to have started the outbreak here a few years back, but no one seems to care a damn.

The country is being run by a government of university educated bods, instead of businessmen and statesmen and this is supposed to be progress!

Since the year 2000, there are only four operational farms in Pertenhall and there are no agricultural labourers, as such, living in the village. There are three or four parcels of land which are farmed by farmers from the adjoining villages.

I have kept in close contact with the village and although there is still no pub or shop, the old primary school has been turned into the village hall and quite a few people have worked hard to provide a meeting place and organise functions, which are essential for newcomers to the village to integrate and enjoy village life.

Children seem to be in short supply, but then maybe they do not go out to play like we used to. Fast traffic and small children are not a safe mix. The television is a big drawing card in the home. I wonder how many there are in the village now – children, not television sets!

There is still the church, but no resident vicar. The Moravian Chapel has gone and there is no Whit Monday Fete to attend, with the lucky-dip bran tub, always a treat for small children and an ice-cream cornet if one was really lucky.

A day trip by coach to Wicksteed Park or Hunstanton was the highlight of the year for many children and memories still linger and not all of them happy ones.

I hope you have enjoyed my trip down memory lane as much as have enjoyed writing it – c'est la vie – Claude.

CHAPTER THREE

Claude's Diaries

The Diaries

Finding myself laid up during my cancer treatment, but still wanting to keep the brain active, I decided to set about 'archiving' Dad's diaries. They were everywhere, in his bureau, in boxes, in bookcases, basically all over the place. So, with the floor covered, I set about putting them in order and counting them. There are 49 diaries in total, beginning in 1953 to the final one in 2017. There are 13 missing, over the years, with a big gap from 1979 – 1985, which is a shame. However, in 1972 Mum's diary survives and this makes an interesting story all of its own.

The last 30 odd years of diaries, I had bought for Dad for his Christmas present. He was always impossible to buy for, either for Christmas or birthdays. You would ask him what he wanted, and he would say, "I don't want anything, I have everything I need!" This also meant that he never went out and bought Christmas or Birthday presents for any of us, including Mum! And he wondered why she didn't talk to him half the time! As we got older, he would ask us to go out and get a present for Mum from him. But she wasn't any better, as she never knew what she wanted and whatever we did come up with, she generally did not want, so it ended up in the 'present cupboard' for recycling and you would often find yourself getting, for your birthday or Christmas, whatever you had bought for Dad to give to Mum, which she did not want!

In fact, I would doubt that Dad ever stepped inside the sort of shop where you could buy a present above ten times in his life! The only shop he visited on a regular basis was Helletts, the butchers. This, more often than not, as Matthew will testify, led to two visits. The first on a Friday to buy the Sunday joint. The second, on the Monday, to go back and complain that this was the worst piece of meat he had ever eaten in his life, and that it was as tough as old boots!

After being assured by Helletts that there was nothing wrong with the meat and no one else had complained; Dad then took the route most men would avoid, by deciding it must be Mum's cooking! This often resulted in a third visit to the butchers to buy a pork pie for his lunch, because Mum had gone on strike!

Everything with Dad lasted well past its usefulness, including, in particular, clothes and memorably, televisions.

When I moved back to the village, Dad would ask if I would come round and watch the football with him. This I was always happy to do, until I quickly realised that you had no idea who was playing or what the score was. The telly was so old that a two-inch thick black line had developed down the left hand side of the screen which completely masked who the teams were and the score, up in the left hand corner. If I came round after the start, I would ask who was playing – he didn't know! What is the score? I think the blue team might be one up!

It was finally decided they needed a new television, and he went down to Watsons to choose one. A great big wide-screened television arrived. Hallelujah! Trouble is, Dad did not know how to work it and he was a 'flicker' with the remote. So at least five times every day (one time when I was away on holiday!) I would get a phone call, "The bloody telly has broken, and you need to get round here and fix it". This generally involved unplugging everything and waiting until it had reset itself and plugging it back in. Sometimes he would do a really good job on it, so that even I could not fix it and poor old David Watson was dragged out to get it going. "Why can't I have my old telly back"!

So, Christmas presents for Dad were easy. An A4 diary with a week to view. A tin of Quality Street. Christmas morning, he would sit and copy everything from the back of 'last year's' diary, so all his shoot dates were in, and January looked very busy!

Claude's Diaries – 1953

I have all dad's early diaries, 1953 – 1978 in a shoe box. Some of the dairies are tiny, but starting at the beginning, the 1953 dairy measures 3 inches by six inches, with 'Levers' Farmers Diary on the cover. I see they were Cattle Food Suppliers, based in Birkenhead, Cheshire.

January 1st does not start until page 35 and the preceding 34 pages make fascinating reading. There is all manner of topics from feeding cattle, as you might expect, but not limited to cows, also covering pigs, sheep and poultry. How to estimate the weight of cattle, with charts on approximate live and dead weight of fat cattle. Two pages of weights and measures, where land is measured in rods, poles or perches and where 4 roods = 1 acre and where 100 acres make a hide, and 40 hides make a barony!

Corn is measured in pottles, pecks and bushels, with 36 bushels making a chaldron!

Then there are periods of gestation for every animal found on a farm, from horse, through to cat. The gestation period for a sow, we are told, is 3 months, 3 weeks and 3 days or 115-120 days. Remember this statistic, as it will be proved later! The remaining pages from 21-34 are Gestation Tables. They start with 'Date of Service', followed by the 'Name of Animal', then 'Due to give birth' and four columns for Mare, Cow, Ewe or Sow.

I see on 22nd March, an entry *(by Dad)* Deaf Sow (serviced), and chart says, due to give birth on 15th July. I thought I must have misread this – Deaf Sow – how would they know? But incredibly, entry in the diary for 15th July – Deaf Sow, 8 pigs, 2 dead. And the incubation period – exactly 115 days, or 3 months, three weeks and 2 days!

The farm was mixed, but predominantly pasture for the cattle and sheep. The pigs lived in hovels! The crops grown were mainly for animal feedstuffs, mangolds, clover, hay and oats. Sugar Beet was also grown, and it would appear were lifted by hand, hard work that! Most crops were sent away on the trains, as lorry loads of everything, even including wool went up to Kimbolton Station and quite often something was picked up off the train at the same time, perhaps a load of chalk for the land. Future big crops for Dad, wheat and potatoes, were grown in much smaller quantities. Potatoes appear to have been grown only for own use, and Snowy (Gentle) and Vic (Roddis), farm labourers, were allowed half a day off to go and dig their own potatoes.

All the cattle and pigs had names, although not much imagination had gone into the naming process, with very few exceptions! Indeed, only one cow had a proper name, 'Jessemine', like the name of the girl in the beautiful song by the Equals in 1964, (I am certain, not named after Dad's cow!) Others, Ginger Cow, Big Roan Cow, Jersey Cow, Thin Red Cow and my favourite 'Pretty Cow'! The pigs did not come off so well in the naming department with some variously named as, Deaf Pig (as we have heard), Wonky Pig and Lame Pig!

The land at Stonely was called the Colleges, as it was rented from one of the colleges in Cambridge. Cattle and sheep were moved from the Colleges to Pertenhall (where the main farm was) and vice-versa. They would have been walked the 2-3 miles, which I am sure was interesting! The cattle and sheep frequently 'got out', down at the Colleges and I bet that was 'fun' rounding them up!

I will talk more about the jobs they did in the 1954 episode, but it was not all work and no play. Dad collected a cricket hut from the Igranic in Bedford, which would have been for Pertenhall CC, he also cut the grass for the OK's (Old Kimboltonian's) cricket match.

On Wednesday, 14th January they had the Lt Staughton shoot, which he calls The Crown Shoot, where they shot 113 head. Two weeks later they only got 55 head!

Rabbit and pigeon shooting were big and on 15th May they caught 30 rats!

2nd June was Coronation Day, and they had the day off. Dad records the weather every day and the weather for that whole week was very wet, so the poor young Queen was not so much reigning over us but raining over us!

On Wednesday 25th November Dad had a lovely day, shooting until early afternoon, then up to Wembley, where I checked the records and saw that he went to see England versus Hungary, where England lost 6-3 and he saw the wonderful Puskas (*the best footballer I ever saw play*) and Stanley Matthews for England.

On Christmas Day he went to watch Bedford Town play Dartford, where Bedford won 4-2 in front of a crowd of 5295 and then on Boxing Day, they played Dartford away, drawing 1-1.

On Boxing Day Dad went to watch Luton Town play West Ham, where they won 3-1, overturning the previous day's result at West Ham, where they had lost 1-0.

What would today's prima donna Premiership footballers make of having to play back-to-back games!

The Diaries 1953 – 1955

Unusually, I am going to start from back to front, with 1955 first. This was the year Mum and Dad married, on 1st June, but strangely there is no mention of the big day, indeed the diary abruptly ends on Thursday 19th May and there are no more entries after that for the rest of the year.

"Borrowed Jimmy's (Cook) muck spreader on seeds.
Fenced round the Hoo (Farm)
6 lambs and 5 sheep to St Neots."

Yet on Thursday 27th January he had recorded *"Nobby's Wedding"* and on Friday 4th February – *"Nobby back to work"*. Nobby – or Bob is Dad's brother.

Back we go to 1954, where, in the blank pages at the front for notes, are some pencil drawings of plans for Mum and Dad's new house, which is to be built on the land at 'The Colleges' at Stonely. The first drawings are very amateurish but turn over the page and he has clearly got to grips with architectural drawings and they fully represent the house as it is now, with the upstairs rooms shown as Main Bedroom, Spare Bedroom, Little Bedroom and Bathroom.

But I panic as I read through the diary for 1954, as despite the plans, there is no mention of the house being built. On 1st December Dad goes up to Wembley to see England play West Germany in a friendly, which the home team wins 3-1. Then, and not before time, on 2nd December they start clearing up the roadway, which would have been a dirt track, from Hatchet Lane in a dogleg, up to where the house is to be built. The next day they are cutting out the roadway, then two loads of rubble come from the aerodrome at Kimbolton, followed two weeks later by more rubble from Islip which now continues apace, with finally on Monday 20th December, *"pegged out the house at the Colleges with John Smith"* (from Gt Staughton). The next day they begin digging out the foundations and, on the Thursday, they finish cementing the footings. Our family home and farmhouse is finally being built.

Originally, Dad told me some years later, his Father was going to buy what we always referred to as 'The Bean's House', which was situated at the end of Hatchett Lane, for Mum and Dad's first home. Mr and Mrs Bean must have been the successful bidders at that time and probably lived there for 50 years. More recently, this cottage, with its extensive garden, was knocked down and there are now 3-4 new build houses, where we once might have lived.

1953 is the year that much of the farm as we know it today begins to come together and I think it is in the winter of 1953-1954 that Dad meets Mum at The Chequers, Eynesbury where Mum was working for her uncle, Terrence Hone, the landlord and where Dad was attending a shoot dinner. I can only surmise, as Dad does not include any personal details in his diaries, whilst football matches, shooting, point-to-points and cricket all feature, even his brother's wedding, but not his own!

In earlier stories I have talked about the animals on the farm, from Cattle to Sheep and Pigs and the jobs feeding them, birthing them and rounding them up when they escaped. I now look at the other jobs on the farm, many of which do not exist now with today's modern farming methods. Dad meticulously records each day's jobs and the diaries in themselves almost read like a novel. He records contractors brought in to do jobs – Farrer brought in to start laying water to 'Winks'. Lee Farrer still does drainage work for us today; was this his father or grandfather referred to? Early January saw a huge amount of threshing going on and 85 sacks of wheat were taken up the station and whilst up there, brought back a ton of rolled barley. The beans and oats also had to be threshed, and on another day a load of wheat was taken to the mill for grinding. Tons and tons of manure was brought in, and this was spread prior to drilling, with it all recorded with the name of the field being worked on, so drilling Grass Field with No 4 corn and No 4 manure and at other times No 6 corn and No 4 manure. Pitchpoled the back field. In January he had gone to Abbotsley to see a demonstration of pitchpoling (I am still not entirely sure what this involved), but after this, they seem to be pitchpoling everywhere! Started clover rubbing, which took three hours, but the seed was no good. On wet days they cleared out places or mended sacks and they seemed to forever be going up to Perry to bring back wood. This was another wet day job, making hurdles for fencing. They seemed to be fencing everywhere at this time and laying new hedges.

New roads were being laid from the Colleges at Stonely right through to the Hoo Farm at Pertenhall. The runways from the airfield at Kimbolton were being broken up and lorry loads of brick, rubble and cement were brought and these still stand testament today, some seventy years later. Those runways which had seen the magnificent Flying Fortresses from the American 379 Bombardment Group depart on their missions over Germany in WW2, now continue to carry our huge farm machinery today. Old air force buildings and equipment were purchased and fashioned for new uses (nothing was wasted in those days) and even into the 1960's you could still see American jeeps driving around.

On 1st May 1953 they dug out a hole at the Pertenhall Farm for the petrol tank. I remember this well as a child. Mum used to take us up the farm to fill up the car.

There was a green metal cabinet with a door and inside a wooden lever for pumping the petrol, in a left to right motion, with the hose which you attached to the petrol tank in the car. At some point during the 1960's the petrol must have become 'red'. This meant it was no longer permitted for domestic use. Mum, never much one for rules and regulations, continued to go up there to fill up the car. I think us kids might have 'dropped her in it' more than once as we reported to Dad that we had seen our cousins when we went up the farm to get petrol. I remember there being 'words' and after a few of these scenes, Mum then reluctantly started getting petrol from Robinsons, in the village, which obviously was not 'free' like up the farm but kept things legal and at least there was a petrol attendant, so she did not have to do all the messy work herself, all be it that the cost must have come out of Mum's housekeeping!

The Livestock

We all know that female pigs are sows and male pigs are boars, similarly sheep are ewes and rams whilst cattle are cows and bulls. However, reading Dad's diaries for 1953 and 1954, I came across words for these animals that I did not recognise and had to look up the definitions.

A hog is a young sheep from 9-18 months of age.

A tup is another word for a ram.

A teg is a 2-year-old sheep.

A female cow does not become a 'cow' until it is around three years of age and has had a calf, before then it is known as a heifer. It can be known as a first calf heifer, when it has had its first birth.

A steer is a nine-month-old male cow. A bullock is a castrated male. They are castrated young enough, to ensure they do not develop bull's characteristics.

A gilt is a female pig which is under one year old.

On 3rd January 1953 6 pigs went to the Ministry. The local unit of the Ministry was the food office which organised the supply of certain foodstuffs, prior to the end of rationing the following year.

The year had not started well, by 4th January, the sheep had already got out at The Colleges (Stonely) three times!

Later that week 55 of last year's lambs were picked out and put on seeds (clover) and the rest were taken up the 'drome', which we assume was Lt.Staughton aerodrome, for grazing. The lambs on seeds were obviously being fattened up as 51 lambs and 6 pigs went off to Bedford market a couple of weeks later and the lambs up the 'drome' were moved onto next piece of grazing land.

Lambing in 1953 started on 12th February and finished on 15th May. Lambing now-a-days would still last this length of time, but it would be more controlled with the tup being put with a group of ewes and the covering dates staggered (and recorded), so the whole flock would lamb at different times and this would be better managed. Back then the tup would be left in a field with the whole flock, to run around and do his stuff, but they would have little idea of when an ewe would actually give birth. Also, the flock was not brought in for lambing, as happens now, so the farmer would get up in the morning and check the flock and see who had lambed overnight. There were a lot of casualties and all was meticulously recorded daily in the diary, for example, *'Sheep had a double, one died. Sheep had a dead single. Three doubles, one single. Black sheep had three lambs. Three doubles, two singles, one single dead, put one of the three on her'.* By 1st March 58 live lambs were recorded. On 17th March, the lambs' tails were cut. This would have been painful for the lambs and in a few years, a plastic ring would be put on the lamb's tails at birth, which cut off the blood supply and a few days later the tail would drop off, painlessly.

Breeding lambs is a labour-intensive business and the next job recorded is 'Clagged 40 tegs', which basically is clearing all the dried-up faeces from round their nether regions, to avoid flies and in the worst cases, maggots.

Shearing then took place of the 'cleaned up tegs' and Jabe (Robbins) and Joe (Roddis) sheared 47 sheep on the Thursday, with shearing completed on the bank holiday Monday. In the meantime, the *'black backed sheep had a 'wonky' lamb'.*

Next job was foot rotting the lambs and finally all the sheep were 'drenched', which today would be known as dipping. All the while, the sheep and lambs were being moved to fresh pastures, walking for some miles from Stonely up to Pertenhall and back.

4th August, Dad seems to have a head count and records 133 lambs, 77 sheep and one ram. Then the whole breeding process soon starts again, as on 29th August, tups are put with the sheep. On 21st September, tups are taken away for a day, (to re gird their loins presumably)!

In 1954 one of the oldest lambs went down with 'pulpy kidney'. A couple of days later, 47 lambs and 30 sheep were inoculated against this disease.

They did not seem to have a lot of luck with the pigs as from an earlier story we can tell they were a poor bunch, variously named, deaf sow, wimpy sow and lame sow. Perhaps to try and improve the breeding stock, a couple of sows were taken up to Joe Bates' to be put with his boar. The pair must have been left at the Bates' as on 3rd November, it is recorded, *'two sows hogged at Joe Bates'.* Meanwhile back at home, *'Sow pigged with 12. Deaf sow pigged, 8 alive, two dead. Two sows pigged, one with 8 and one with 13, ended up with 8 each.'*

Casualties or fallen stock were regularly recorded and these were taken for disposal at Tebbutts in Eynesbury.

For the most part, the cattle seemed to calve without too much drama and were recorded as *'Pretty Cow calved'* and in brackets either an (H) for Heifer or (B) for a Bull. Sadly, 'Jersey Cow' calved, but died two weeks later. Presumably, the calf was hand reared, although not recorded.

When it was time to sell stock, unless it was going to the Ministry, fattened cattle, sheep, or pigs went to Bedford market, generally on a Saturday, but occasionally Kettering market was used, which was held on a Thursday.

Finally, in December 1954, electric fencing was employed to keep the cattle in. This was well before the days of 'health and safety' and the voltage going through the electric fencing, was pretty strong, as I can confirm. We know what happens you are told, "Whatever you do, don't touch the electric fence!" The cattle were great escape artists, frequently getting themselves out and walking several miles to find new pasture and one can only image the devastated crops in their wake!

Slim Pickings – The 1960's Diaries

Only four diaries from this decade have survived and they are of the small pocket type, all written in pencil, with the pencil and diary always kept in Dad's pocket, no wonder they are so battered! Indeed the 1966 diary looks as though it might have 'fallen in the drink' as many of the pages are stuck together! The 1965 and 1966 diaries came from S.V.Robinson's Garage, Kimbolton and the 1968 and 1969 diaries are farming diaries from Offord and Buckden Mills and a spraying firm, Heygates Chemicals.

Despite their tiny size, these four diaries hold a wealth of information about farming in the 1960's. They contain everything from weather reports, although Dad wasn't measuring rainfall yet, as he would in later years, the farm labourers' hours worked and so much more. The men would be paid an hourly rate for drilling, setting potatoes, hoeing, ditching and hedging and wet day jobs, sweeping up the yard and painting. They worked a five-and-a-half-day week and overtime was paid, particularly during harvest. There was also piece work, where, for example, the men were paid for every net of brussels sprouts or sack of potatoes picked.

Throughout the diaries there are huge columns of figures tallied – there were no calculators back in those days and he also does some really complicated long division sums. Then against all these entries are ticks in biro, where all the figures are transferred to his farm accounts books, ready for the day, once a month, when the farm secretary would call. This was always a wet weather job for Dad, and we would get told, "Don't disturb your dad, he is doing the booking".

Importantly the diaries record who the goods went away to, on Wednesday 17th February 1965 there were 70 sprouts to Darlow, 70 to Wagers and 100 to Barbers and 20 to F. Bayes. That is 260 nets of brussels sprouts picked by three men in two days and before breakfast on the third day, before the orders were collected. Some 85 nets picked each man, by hand, very hard, back breaking work with hands red from the cold and chilblains, standing in mud and wearing plastic leggings to try and keep their bottom half dry. Then back next day for more of the same. The men did get some days off, as brassicas cannot be picked in frosty weather. You can imagine a net of picked frosted brussels sprouts, as soon as they get warm, they will begin to smell and then rot, before they even reach the shelves. If there were too many days of frosty weather, then the price of brussels sprouts would rocket – market forces, and as Dad records in January 1968 – *'deep snow – no men at work'*. Next day – *'heavy frost, Peter, Dick and Alf did not come in – no picking'*.

In 1965 they finished picking sprouts on 24th March, then the following week all three men had the week off. They came back first week of April for a full week of planting potatoes and autumn sprouts and so the cycle begins again. This year they also grew beetroot and swede. It was also around this time that Mum got hold of a second-hand Walls ice cream freezer, which was kept in the garage. Domestic freezers were not really a thing back then. This certainly improved the variety of our vegetables during the winter, as prior to this, it was brussels sprouts with everything. I still cannot eat them to this day! However, at the start, Mum seemed to mix two forms of preserving foods and would heavily salt, blanche and then freeze bags and bags of runner beans, which she grew in the garden. The monotony of brussels sprouts was then relieved by extremely salty runner beans, until she soon realised that just the blanching would suffice!

The diaries were also used as a 'sprayer, drilling and fertilising manual', with instructions to himself as to how to set the machine up, for example, *'Dexta – Row crop wheels at 60". Disks facing in, wheels narrow way with nuts outwards.'* *'Spraying DDT on drilled sprouts against the Flea Beetle – 4 pints makes 50 gallons,'* or *'spraying Avadex near house, 35 Fergusson, 4th gear, 30lb pressure, 20 gallons to the acre'.* For the farmer, centuries of only being able to get rid of pests and weeds by hoeing, meant that when the chemical sprays started to come to market, they were of the pretty lethal variety. Everything pretty much had skull and crossbones on it and as kids we were told, "Don't go near the spray or granules. Don't touch it. Don't touch your face or eyes." I don't know how we survived!

June-August were the busy months of the year, with the potato crop coming ready, just as the fields of wheat and barley needed harvesting. So, it was all hands to the deck, with even us kids mucking in and picking potatoes. We got paid the same rate per bag as the men, but obviously we were not such quick pickers. We got paid on a Friday, same as the men and we felt so rich! Before we started, we had quite a lecture from Dad as to which potatoes to pick. We must not pick the small potatoes which were like marbles, (those got eaten at home, together with the potatoes which had been damaged by the potato harvester), no damaged or diseased potatoes, no mud and definitely no stones! Very occasionally a load would be returned, and Dad took this very personally and I can still remember the eruption and language! But this cannot have been entirely unexpected as he had recorded in the diaries, *'King Edwardes in Monts, small and blighty'* or *'Started lifting at the Farm – hopeless. No weight and scabby as hell'*. Dad always inspected the rows us kids had been picking. We must have annoyed the hell out of the farm workers, constantly asking them, "Is this potato alright?" If we had missed too many (borderline quality), we would get a right ticking off, we could not win!

I love his weather comments and spring 1969 must have been very wet as on 13th March, Dad writes, *'Rain all night. Floods at mid-day deepest since 1952'*. And in May – *'heavy rain for part of the week, with thunder and hailstorms making the land impossible once again'*. Or a forlorn, *'Land now in a deplorable condition. Prospects of seedtime and harvest seem far away'*.

But it was not all work and no play, and this is not recorded in his 1966 diary, but Dad had tickets for all five of England's World Cup matches, at Wembley, up to and including the semi-finals. I remember this, as we were taking our annual one week's summer holiday at Clacton-on-Sea and on Wednesday, 20th July, Dad left us at the hotel with Mum and caught the train from Clacton, down to London, to see England beat France 2-0 with Roger Hunt scoring both the goals.

Life on the Farm 1970 – 1974

We move into **1970** and, to give context, Dad is 44 years old and has been married for 15 years. He is still writing in these tiny, tiny diaries, which are, despite their size, packed full of detail. Here are some of the best bits to give a flavour of farming and life at this time.

The diaries continue to be an important spraying manual, with for example, *'Avadex on Big Field, red nozzles, 4th gear, 27lb pressure, puts 20 gallon per acre at 4 and half mph'*.

At the beginning of April, *'Jock had his cards after playing up for a couple of months'*. I think Dad was quite a hard task master, but fair, I hope, as he records religiously, when the men did not come in or wanted a day off, or, God forbid, a week off! Then recording, Dick has two days holiday left.

There were times though when the weather dictated what work could be done and I sense the frustration as he writes on 11th April – *'no work on the land since 2nd April. Misty and damp and everybody fed up'*. I think probably Dad was the most fed up!

In **1971** (21.25 inches) Dad begins recording daily rainfall, which is then carried forward to monthly and finally giving an annual figure for the year.

8th April – *'have got the bug – very unpleasant'*. Dad was dreadful when he was ill – not a good patient!

21st June – *'saw the first bolters in sugar beet.'* This is when the odd beet would go to seed, without putting down the crop – obviously you do not want too many of these.

1st November – *'putting shoddy on at Stonely'*. Shoddy was a form of fertilizer used back then. I believe it was waste material from the wool and cotton mills and 'material' being the operative word. The fields were covered in this brightly coloured material waste and until ploughed in, it looked a dreadful mess, as though everywhere had been covered in litter.

1972 (17.1 inches) This is an interesting year, as we have two diaries to study, the second one being Mum's Diary, which I will leave for a special story of its own! So 'Dad's Diary' for this year is a bit thin! On Saturday 12th August they *'began lifting potatoes and they had a useful yield, but there was too much rubbish in the crop for a top yield.'*

1st September he records, *'have had 18 days combining in a row, uninterrupted by the weather, have only one day left to do. Very good yields and top-quality grain'*.

1973 (17.6 inches) Nothing else to report! Mum must have been running another diary, which has not survived!

1974 (23.92 inches) Tuesday 8th January, they were shooting at The Crown, Little Staughton and Dad records 91 head, including 14 and half brace of partridges. There were gale force winds (which would have made the birds fly) and torrential rain (which would have kept the birds on the ground) in the afternoon. The two weathers cancelling out the flying conditions! However, the meal for 18 in the evening at The Crown cost £39.86

Interestingly, the bags recorded at this time are almost identical to those currently being achieved, 119 head, 85 head, 76 head, including 18 and half pheasant, 14 partridges, hare, pigeon etc. Pretty normal bag here, but one year they managed to shoot a sea gull. Poor bird, miles from the sea and in the wrong place at the wrong time! The gun who brought down the nautical species took a bit of ribbing! Back then Roger Dunkley reared all the birds that were put down, in breeding pens at the back of his pub, The White Horse, Tilbrook. If we had a hen (fowl) which had gone 'broody', she would be rounded up and taken up to Roger, who would sit her on a clutch of pheasant eggs. These hens made good 'pheasant mothers!'

On 4th February, in Mum's handwriting, crocuses out in the rose bed.

3rd March, Dad was cutting the cricket square.

Sad one here – on 20th April, my sister's much loved first pony, Misty, was sold to the Williams' of Pertenhall Manor.

Dad's diaries from now on record all the 'firsts', so on 21st April he saw his first blackbird and the following day, heard the Cuckoo for the first time. On 1st May the cherry tree in the garden was in full bloom.

31st May was Aunt Nell's funeral – born in 1885 – this wonderful maiden Aunt was, I believe, the last person to be buried at the Moravian Chapel at the top of Pertenhall Hill.

The precariousness of farm prices is illustrated in just one week in July, where on 2nd Dad records, potatoes down to £50 a ton. By the 5th they had rallied to £66 a ton, but by 9th had dropped to £30 a ton.

On 27th October they are lifting Sugar Beet at Stonely, where he records a very poor crop. Gappy beet, no size and low sugar content (14.3).

18th November and I remember this well, floods worse than any time since 1968. Chadwell Lane, Pertenhall have had a cover of water 2-3 feet high all day. He then forlornly states that *'it could be a month before work starts again'*. However, for us kids, floods meant earning pocket money! We would go down to the bottom of the Bedford Road, in Stonely, where the River Kim had burst its banks. Cars trying to drive through to Kimbolton from St. Neots would inevitably conk out in the middle of the flood and the drivers were always 'happy' to give us kids, (who just happened to be hanging around), between 10p if they were mean to 50p if they were rich, to push their cars out. We generally went home with our wellies full of water (and pockets full of coins) – which a bit of rolled up newspaper soon dried out!

This must have been a bad year for farm prices, as on 28th November Dad records that they had to stop picking sprouts at 11.30am as the prices had dropped to their lowest for 20 years, in his experience. I am sure the greater rainfall for this year – more than six inches of rain to the year before, must have had a bearing on everything from state of the soil, to yields and the farmers' mood.

However, it was not all doom and gloom, as on the day before, Dad had gone to George Peck's shoot, and he notes that they shot 129 head and that it was his 'Best Day's Shooting Ever'!

CHAPTER FOUR

World War 2 – Claude's Version of Events!

The Evacuees

Claude came from that generation where the Second World War was still a big thing and as we would say now, "B.C. – Before Christ" or "A.D. – After Christ" – with Dad everything was always "Before the War" or "After the War". And whilst the War lasted six years, if you were a boy of 13 when it started and a man of 19 when it finished, this was a big thing to happen during your formative years. Perhaps the only comparable event in recent years will be Covid and it will probably be spoken of as "Before Covid" or "After Covid". This story was amongst a folder of 'unpublished stories' my sister found whilst clearing out her office. It is likely that Dad had taken them to her for typing and she had never got round to it. This story Dad had entitled – 'Short history of the part the people of Pertenhall played in the successful conclusion of the second world war 1939 – 1945.' Around the same time, in November 2005, Dad had been recorded by the BBC for an oral history of WW2 entitled, "The Peoples War", which had taken place at Risely Village Hall. I have the transcript of the recording, which was strangely entitled "Aniseed balls and the missing

Cannon"! Many of the events appear in the story and the interview and I will try and do justice to World War 2 according to Claude!

I was born on 25th January 1926, so I was 13, going on 14 in September 1939. My mother had died when I was about three years old, and I went to live with my grandmother and grandfather up at Manor Farm in Pertenhall. It was unlucky that my mother died, but I think it was the best thing that happened, because I had a really happy childhood up there on the big farm.

Adolf Hitler's Nazi Party had gained control of Germany in the early 1930's and very soon began to re-arm, in contravention of their surrender agreement following the end of the 1914-1918 war. Hitler was a fanatic and he surrounded himself with like-minded militants with the aim to conquer the world. The German people, with the defeat of WW1 still fresh in their minds, were whipped up by Hitler's impassioned speeches, suggesting that they were 'the master race' and what their country needed was guns, not butter. He sent some of his airforce to help the insurgents fight in the Spanish Civil War, which taught them some of the tricks of the trade when the blitzkrieg started in 1940.

Germany started to gobble up their smaller neighbouring countries, but when they invaded Poland, Britain and France realised that Hitler could not be appeased and must be opposed. In hindsight, war had been inevitable for at least a couple of years and so it was, on Sunday 3rd September, as war clouds loomed, we had been told to go to church and as we left church that morning, a lady called Sue Bates, who lived in a bungalow opposite the church, came running up the path saying, "We are at War with Germany". I think quite honestly that we all went "phew" – thank goodness for that, because politicians had been talking about this war for two years and it had got to the stage where they thought it would never happen.

But at the same time, plans to evacuate London had been in readiness for some time and so on the evening of Monday 4th September, we found ourselves waiting up at the school at Pertenhall for our evacuees to arrive from Walthamstow. Of course, we all stood scanning the B660, the road from Bedford to Kimbolton and time kept shuntering on and it started to get dusk, when all of a sudden, we heard these buses coming from Risely way and instead of one bus, there were two buses. The first bus was empty, they had already dropped off some evacuees at Risely and Swineshead. The second bus stopped opposite the school gate and the bus door opened and these young women with small children started getting off. They had all got labels around their necks, they looked like they were items that were up for sale. The last person to get off the bus, well she actually never really got right off the bus, was an old lady all dressed in black, with a black hat on. She said, as she had got one foot on the ground and one foot still on the bus, "How far is the nearest pub?" And somebody said, "Well the Kangeroo is a mile and the Chequers at Keysoe is a mile and a half and there's two pubs in Kimbolton, but that's two miles". "Oh bugger that!" said the old lady, "I'd rather face the German bombers than live in a village without a pub" and with that she got back on the bus!

The winter of 1939-1940 was what became known as the phoney war, nothing much was happening. The evacuation arrangements had been put in hand because of what everyone had expected, assuming that the minute war was declared, there would be 500 bombers flying over London, dropping bombs and everyone would be blown to smithereens. The evacuees, during that winter, got so fed up they could not stick it in the country. Everything was so different for them, and they gradually migrated back to Walthamstow, with only the odd one or two that stayed.

Those that Served

The following are a list of names of people from Pertenhall who served in the second world war. Sadly, the two who lost their lives must head the list and they are as follows.

Jack Bennett from the Kangeroo – R.A.F.

Frank Wilson from Sunnyside Farm. He was in digs at the farm, but worked as a keeper on the Kimbolton Estate – Army

Stancy Banks (my sister) and Peggy Squirrel, school friends who both enlisted in the Army and served in the ATS

Annie Presland – WAAF

Douglas Lock and his brother Ian were in the R.A.F. before the war. They quite often flew over Pertenhall, doing aerobatics at low level, which upset quite a few local people and the farm animals, in particular the working horses.

Bert Bates and Bill Presland were both called up early in the war because they were both of an age that no exemption was allowed, which was called the Militia.

Jim and Cyril Clark were enlisted into the Army and Jim served in the Far East and was probably lucky to escape intact.

Bill Dawson and Tommy Hardwick both served in the Army.

John Shelton joined the R.A.F. towards the end of the war and Spencer Leflay joined the Navy round about the same time.

Frank Condliffe joined the Army.

Ernest McClelland joined the R.A.F. and was shot down over Germany early in the war and spent the rest of the time in a prisoner of war camp.

This was a big percentage of the working population of Pertenhall and made the running of the farms more difficult, especially as most of the grassland had to be ploughed up and brought back into production to help feed the nation.

I was eager to sign up and do my bit for the Country. As soon as I reached the age of 17, I caught the bus to Bedford one Saturday. I went to the enlisting office and volunteered for the Services. The guy in an Army uniform behind the desk remarked that it was very noble of me to volunteer (his words, not mine!) He enquired as to my name, my address and my job. When I told him that I drove a tractor on my father's farm, he put down his pen, looked me in the eye and said, "Go back home and get on your tractor and work as hard as you can. This country at the moment (end of January 1943) has exactly three weeks of food supplies left. The U-boats are sinking ships faster than they can be built and we are more likely to be starved into submission, than beaten by a better army of men". I have never forgotten those words and I left the office feeling pleased that I was still doing my bit for the Country.

Growing up during the War

It was said that the first two bombs dropped in Bedfordshire exploded on open land up the Swineshead Road, close to Grange Farm, where my school friend John Shelton lived. The first bomb broke a few windows in their house and the second dropped in the adjoining field. This was in October 1939, and I can remember me and John picking up some of the shrapnel left behind and then taking it to Kimbolton School, where we were being educated and selling a few of the bits to the boarders!

Various types of air-raid shelters became available, one a kind of metal table for indoors, called a Morrison shelter. One for outdoors was called an Anderson shelter and this was a domed metal affair which could be buried in the garden, with access down steps and through a metal door. On heavy soil, these shelters tended to fill up with water, but probably did save lives in the towns.

Mr Pelham of Wood End House became the head of the ARP (Air Raid Precautions) and Will Peppitt and Jack Fincher became A.R.P. wardens. Among their duties were to see that no light could be seen at night through windows, with "black-out curtains" being one of the most used phrases in local conversation. One night one of the A.R.P. wardens knocked on our door and my stepmother went to answer it. "Would you please get your clothes in off the line, because the German planes might see them when they fly over and drop a bomb on them!" I think it was because he lived quite close to our farm, and he was worried about it. Motor car headlights were fitted with a grill to cut down the glare that might be seen from an enemy aircraft.

We started having Air Raid Precautions lectures at the school in Pertenhall. I was about 14 years old at the time and I was so keen to be in on all of this! We used to look forward to these lectures because the old guy who did the talks was named Woodcock and I think he came from Little Staughton, or somewhere. The reason why we were so keen to go was because instead of calling these bombs 'incendiary bombs' (the ones that caught everything on fire) – he could not pronounce 'incendiary' and used to call them 'incidenary bombs' and he never ever did get it right! I think that is what captured our imagination! A Fire Watching rota was formed, but I was not old enough to get on it. My Dad was on it, but he got so fed up with being on duty with these two old guys, who were so boring, that he said, "You might as well go in my place," and I did!

The Army had a searchlight near "Hoo Farm", and it made a rendezvous for some of us boys of an evening to have a cup of cocoa and a few biscuits with the soldiers that operated it. I don't ever remember us kids spotting any enemy aircraft when we were up there, but the beam of light was pretty formidable and together with others around the neighbouring villages, made an exciting spectacle not to be forgotten. During the Blitz on London, it was possible to see the bomb bursts and the anti-aircraft fire from The Hoo and it made a lie of the old saying that "Distance lends enchantment".

When we got to May 1940, the news began to get worrying as the Germans decided to let loose their army through France and Belgium. Everyone thought that the Maginot Line would stop the Germans, but before we knew it, they had outflanked that and raced towards the channel ports.

I remember we were having a history lesson at school and the history master, Kyffin Owen said, "We won't talk about history today, because history is being made at this very moment. The German troops are coming through France at the speed of a motorbike, and they will soon be at the Channel coast and quite what will happen, I do not know! They may invade this Country; I just don't know. We will just have to see how things go". This wakened everybody up! We got our troops back from Dunkirk, where they were rescued by a flotilla of little boats and brought back home.

A few days after the fall of France, in June 1940, evacuation of civilians from the South and East coasts took place. A whole school of pupils from New Haven came to Pertenhall and were billeted around the village. Most houses had one or two children, at our farm we had a brother and a sister, and the school master was billeted opposite us. For the most part they integrated extremely well, and were no different to the Pertenhall boys, hardworking and one, Ken Gentle, became one of my best friends. Some children took longer to settle and two boys in another cottage quite close to us, one of the poor little chaps used to wet the bed, when he was 10 years old, but I suppose that is something that happens when you are wrenched away from your parents, as many poor children were all over the Country.

Dad's Army

The Country was now preparing itself for an invasion by the Germans in the late summer or early autumn of 1940. Every village in the land had to organise what was known at the time as the L.D.V. – Local Defence Volunteers. General Lock of the Manor at Pertenhall, a retired Army Officer, who had seen service in India during peacetime, assumed command. He was not unlike Captain Mainwaring of 'Dad's Army' either in looks or behaviour, although I don't think he was quite as bumptious as Captain Mainwaring, but very much the same and indeed Captain Mainwaring could have been modelled on General Lock! The name of Local Defence Volunteers did not inspire enough urgency for the Prime Minister, Mr. Churchill and it was soon renamed 'The Home Guard'. General Lock was very much the right sort of chap to be the Head of the Home Guard.

General Lock sent out an order that every able-bodied male over the age of 16 years old had to report to the school and although I was only 14 years old at the time, I was never far away from the action. Sid Shelton and Tom Bates were made Sergeants and Charlie Weller a Corporal. Most of the members had a 12-bore shot gun and some cartridges were produced with one solid ball of metal (ball bearing) as the projectile. Each member had one box of 25 cartridges, but what would have happened to many of the guns if a shot was discharged, I dread to think! Thankfully they were never put to use. About this time the fire watching rota was organised, but I only remember it being put to the test on one occasion, when a 'bread-basket' (a collective name) of incendiary bombs dropped in the vicinity of the church about midnight in the early autumn of 1941 and one went through the roof of the gardener's cottage at The Manor, occupied by the Weller family.

As the time of the expected invasion got ever closer, various ploys were put in place to slow the enemies advance, if it happened. Trenches were dug either side of the Bedford Road, from below where the council houses are now to the corner near the Manor. Old farm implements were put ready to block the road if need be. Thankfully they were never put to the test.

In preparation, the Home Guard were taken to Clapham gravel pits, where they had got a firing range. They all had a turn with the rifles and so I was really keen to hear how my father had got on when he got back. "How did you get on Dad?" I asked. "Not very well", Dad replied. I knew my dad to be a very good shot and I could not understand how he was not one of the best. Dad told me that he had shot badly on purpose because, "I don't intend to be in the front line when the Germans come. The best shots will get in the front line". I was 14 at the time and Dad was 40 and I can now have a better understanding of the situation, but at the time I noted that it wasn't 'if' the Germans come, but 'when' the Germans come, and I think that was telling.

The crunch came on the Saturday evening, when the London docks had been set on fire by almost 24 hours of continuous bombing by the Luftwaffe. It was early September 1940, and the Home Guard were called out to man the trenches. For some reason Mr Pelham was in charge of the troops, perhaps General Lock was awaiting news at The Manor via the telephone. Having divided the men into two groups, one for each side of the road and having given instruction for no cigarettes to be smoked, Mr Pelham, using a torch, like an usherette at the cinema, directed the men to their positions in the dark, shining the light along the trenches. Herbie Stewart said, "Well Mr Pelham, if we are not allowed to smoke, you can either put that light out, or I am going home!" Mutiny in the ranks! In those days, all these farm workers smoked 20 Woodbines a day, that was the only thing that kept them going and being told not to smoke put them in a bad mood.

As I was not there, because I was not old enough to join, this story came to me second hand, but it is true and caused some light relief in what was a very tense situation. Of course, we know now, the invasion did not take place, but that is due to "The Few" – the young pilots who flew the Hurricanes and Spitfires which stopped the Luftwaffe in 1940 and without them, the Germans would have come and I very much doubt if we could have withstood the threat.

My First Job

A particularly vivid memory is 14th November 1940, the night the Germans bombed Coventry. It was a very moonlight night and around 10 or 11 o'clock in the evening, we all went out and stood in Chadwell Lane to hear the German planes going over. It was just one continual drone, going backwards and forwards.

Towards the end of 1941, Italian prisoner of war labour became available. They were based at Ducks Cross Camp at Colmworth and a telephone call to the camp would

In the years when our Country

was in mortal danger

CLAUDE HENRY CHARLES BANKS

who served 15th February 1943 – 31st December 1944

gave generously of his time and

powers to make himself ready

for her defence by force of arms

and with his life if need be.

George R.I.

THE HOME GUARD

Claude's Home Guard Certificate.

ensure the number of men needed for the next day's work on the farm. They were delivered by lorry at about 8.30am and collected at about 5pm. The cost per hour was less than normal farm worker's wages and most of them proved very willing and able. I do remember one time that we were riddling potatoes when they turned up one morning. This particular gang of prisoners just would not work, and I could not get them to get going. The next day I thought of a fiendish plan, I said, "You chaps, when we get six ton bagged up, you can pack up and do whatever you like for the rest of the day". We got the six ton bagged up by dinner (lunch) time the next day and they had brought a football with them. We all played football together until it was time for the lorry to come – that was good fun, that was! After a few months, any farmer with suitable accommodation could have P.O.Ws to live on the farm. As we had an empty cottage at the time, Dad selected two of the best Italians, both of whom in civilian life were married and had experience of livestock and they were billeted on our farm. They stayed with us until they were repatriated at the end of the war. They never gave us any trouble and worked hard, which gave lie to the myth that Italian men were lazy.

I remember one night, I think it must have been about November 1941, it was a Thursday evening, I know that, because my father had been to St. Neots market, and he always used to bring us back a treat for high tea. This particular time he had brought some smoked haddock and we just sitting down to tuck in at around 6.15pm when we were suddenly aware of this German plane going round. You could always tell the sound of a German plane, because I think they had got a different number of cylinders to the English planes and they made a sort of humming sound, rather than the regular beat that the English planes had. The German plane dropped this stick of six bombs at Keysoe Brook End, which was about a mile and a half from us. There was a sort of a pause of a split second as each bomb hit the ground and exploded. I think if there had been two more bombs in the stick, other than the six, I think my father would have been under the table, because he had readied himself to get under the table. We had a paraffin lamp (no electricity in those days) and this lamp started to sway. That was not a very nice moment, that one!

I left school at Christmas 1941, and they sent me away to work in an Auctioneers office at Thrapston. There was some talk that I always had plenty to say for myself, so perhaps I could cut it doing the auctioning at the cattle market! Or perhaps it was because farming was going downhill fast before the war, and they wanted to get me in some other business. Whatever the reason, I was so dreadfully unhappy, being stuck in an office. I felt as if I was like a wild sparrow, caught in a cage and I just wanted to be outside, doing what I had always been used to doing. One memory from that miserable time, Thrapston was close to the USAF Grafton Underwood Base. Around June time, the base finally became operational for these massive B17s to go and bomb Germany. One night three or four truckloads of these Airmen came to Thrapston, to paint the town red! The next day when the park keeper was going round tidying up the park, he found a pair of lady's knickers and an American gas mask in close proximity! Both were obviously surplus to requirement at the time!

The Harvest Pies

Rationing started early in the war, but country people, by and large, are good managers and larders were well stocked at the beginning, although towards the end, things started to get a bit tight. There was always a rabbit to help with the meat ration, which had gone down to 10d worth of meat per person at one time. Many families in the country kept a pig in a sty down the garden and fed it on household scraps and a little barley meal and when the time was right, the porker was turned into ham and bacon. Friends then appeared that no one had known before! Jams and chutneys, bottled fruits, runner beans salted in earthenware jars, eggs pickled in icing-glass and clamped potatoes, beetroot and carrots, helped the sprouts and cabbage provide vegetables for all occasions.

There was another treat available, and this was not on rations, it was called "Harvest Pie". These were supplied to the village from I know not where, and I think Mr. Pelham had the job of distribution. The employer, obviously in Pertenhall these were the farmers who had to supply the names of those working hard enough to be allowed an allocation. Bill and Vic Roddis were working for us at the time and were able to have their share. This only happened once a week and when the next Thursday came round, I asked Bill if he wanted a ticket for a Harvest Pie and he said that he did not. The reason he gave was that when he had cut the top off the last one, he said that a sheep's eye was looking at him and that it had rather put him off Harvest Pies from then on!

Sobering Times

History shows that although America did not join the war until they had been attacked by Japan at Pearl Harbour on 6th December 1941. By early 1942 the airfields in this region were being prepared for the B17s – The Flying Fortresses, the supposedly impregnable American bombers, which would carry out the daylight raids over German, whilst our boys in Lancasters bombed by night. I do not know which was the most effective, but they both suffered fearful losses and the names read out on Remembrance Sunday are always someone's son, husband, father or grandfather.

To see some of the American planes limp back from raids, with engines stopped and lumps missing from some of the wings was a most sobering experience. Many of them as young 18 or 19 year old danced with the girls at the Mandeville Hall or played darts in the Chequers Inn at Keysoe and the next day, they would be four miles up in the sky facing death or glory and if they got home safely, they would have to do it all again in a few days time. I was not envious of their popularity with the local females. These boys looked very smart in their uniforms, they had nylon stockings, plenty of chocolate, Lucky Strike, Camel and Styvesant cigarettes to give away and I did not blame the girls either; how could I, when my sister Stancy married a Canadian airman from the base at Lt Gransden and a nicer guy than him would be hard to find.

In about April 1943, one of our aircraft cut the top clean off an elm tree up the Swineshead Road. What I think was happening was that they were practicing low flying in preparation for the attack on the dams in Germany, later known as the Dam Buster Raid. If the plane had been another yard or two lower, it would have been brought down. As it was, it had cut about 15 foot off the top of the tree, cut it off, just as if it had been done by a giant knife, with all the leaves and branches left lying in the road.

By now, long range aircraft, with built in radar equipment were beginning to be able to locate the U-boats, when they surfaced to recharge their batteries and from around July 1943, more ships were getting through with supplies. One factor which helped enormously, but probably was not appreciated at the time, but throughout the war we had remarkable weather every summer and the farmers were able to gather in bumper harvests. It seemed that the Lord was on our side, but everything in nature gets evened up and the harvest weather of 1946 was the worst in my memory and the big freeze-up of 1947 meant that farming took a long time to recover.

Finally, in December 1943 Dad agreed for me to come back on the farm. For two years I had been living during the week in Ringstead with relatives of my grandmother, Uncle Lou and Aunt Maria and would cycle to work at Bletsoes in Thrapston. In the summer I would cycle home, to Pertenhall, on a Saturday afternoon, when we finished work and back on a Sunday night. In the winter Dad would pick me up and drop me back. Whether on those journeys he realised just how unhappy I was, I don't know, but finally he said, "I have been thinking, you may as well come back on the farm".

Preparations for D-Day

As 1944 got underway, all the talk was of our forces invading Europe and overthrowing the German regime. In mid-April we awoke one morning at Chadwell Farm to find that the whole place had been taken over by an army motorised division. There were tanks, Bren gun carriers, jeeps and all the paraphernalia of war. They were on practice manoeuvres and were all over Kimbolton and the surrounding area. Obviously, they were preparing for D-Day and with the benefit of hindsight, the woods, narrow lanes and streams around here would not be unlike the territory they would come across after landing on the beaches of Normandy and pushing inland. The snag was, we had remaining in the rickyard, one lovely stack of wheat, all ready to thresh and I suppose some of the soldiers had never seen one in their entire life, let alone know how it might burn if it was exposed to a flame. I was up Swineshead Road at work that morning, when one of our farm workers wives came up to me on her bicycle and told me that the stack was on fire. By the time I got back, the army had scarpered, and Kimbolton Fire Brigade were on the scene. The stack was ruined and had to be taken to pieces, sheaf by sheaf and doused with water. The other men, plus Dad, were working down at Stonely, but the road from there was so blocked with army vehicles, that it took them a long time to reach Chadwell Farm, although by then there was nothing that could be done to save the burning stack.

One of the duties of Pertenhall Home Guard was to guard the railway tunnel at Souldrop. The tunnel was about a mile long and was on the main L.M.S. railway line, the main link through the country up to Scotland. In the build up to the invasion of Europe, it was thought that this tunnel was a likely target for sabotage, because by blowing up this tunnel, this would stop troops being able to be moved up and down the country. Obviously, there were two ends of the tunnel to be guarded, and there were 14 men on each shift and the turn for the Pertenhall Home Guard came round every 10 days. It was summertime and the shifts were nine pm until midnight, midnight until 3am and 3am until 6am.

I usually went on duty with my friend Ken Gentle and on one particular night, we were on the first shift and were told that between 11.30pm and midnight, a Policeman will walk the line from Sharnbrook direction, "To check and see if you guys are awake. Make sure you are waiting for him", we were told. Sure enough, towards the end of our shift that night, we could hear footsteps coming on the gravel along the line from a long way off. When the footsteps got to about 50 or 60 yards away from us, I shouted, "Halt, who goes there?" But the footsteps kept on coming, so I slammed a round up the spout of my rifle and at the click in the stillness of the night, the footsteps stopped, and a voice said, "I am the Policeman, you should have known I was coming". I said, "You should have said who you were, you are lucky you haven't been shot!" He said, "Oh it's alright, you are awake, I'll go on back".

Me and Ken Gentle were on duty the night before D-Day took place. Several Red Cross trains headed south that night and that gave us a good idea that the invasion was imminent.

V.E.Day

Finally, the War in Europe ended in early May 1945. My mate, Ken Gentle and myself had a stroke of luck. We had started playing football for Kimbolton and every registered football club in the Country was allocated a pair of Cup Final Tickets. Everybody's name went in the hat and me and Ken were lucky enough to win the tickets. However, somebody who was a real fan of Charlton Athletic, one of that year's finalists, was desperate to get these two tickets. He had to barter us for them, and eventually the deal was agreed; he offered to put the three of us up, in London, for two or three days, so we could join the "VE Day" celebrations and he would get the Cup Final tickets. So, the three of us had a buckshee place to stay in London for three days. We went up there with quite a bit of money, I don't know about quite a bit – but a few bob anyway!

We had a hell of a time up there; I think actually that I had the best time of my life! Being country lads, we did not know a lot about what went on in the towns. We used to whizz about on the tube trains, visiting different people that we knew who lived in London. At night we went to the Streatham Locarno, a massive great dance hall, which must have held at least 1000 and we danced all night. Then there were all these parties up there, in Trafalgar Square. We were right in the heart of it! We were there!

It was – I still cannot describe it – fantastic – everybody was so happy the war had finished – the war to end all wars.

But of course, it wasn't the war to end all wars, because, I mean, they are still fighting now aren't they? People being killed and all that.

But we did have a hell of a time! We did, that is for sure, and we stopped up there until we ran out of money!

Dad, Mum and friends loved to go to Twinwoods at Clapham for the annual Glenn Miller Concert. Here seen with Henry and Beryl Banks, John and Heather Gowing, Ian and Pat Brown, the inimitable Roger Dunkley and of course, Claude and Daphne Banks.

CHAPTER FIVE

Sport

Sports Day

Wednesday 2nd June 1937. Kimbolton School Under 12's 220 yards handicap.

Sports Day, the 200 yards Under-12 Final. Claude coming a plucky third.

Kimbolton School annual Sports Day was a huge event in the school calendar, with hundreds of parents and friends of the school attending. Distinguished guests were there to present the prizes, and in this year Lord and Lady Lilford did the honours, with former England cricketer, Jack Hobbs and Mr T. R. Parker, who was the school football team coach, a recent manager of Norwich City and current manager of Southampton F.C., and formerly an Arsenal player, were both referees for the day.

The opening event of Sports Day was always the sight of the whole school, in their white kit, providing a display of the 'Swedish Drill', a gymnastic exercise regime which the boys carried out with smartness and precision, as they worked through the 16 exercises. In later years they would perfect the human pyramid!

In 1933 Harold Abrahams, 100 metres Olympic champion from 1924, was there to present the prizes. In this year, the Obstacle Race was ingeniously arranged to represent 'a day in school life' and amongst other things the competitors had to, 'work out sums on a blackboard, bowl at a set of stumps, don pyjamas and light a candle'!

We learn from the newspaper reports that the School 'Houses' were named, Squirrels, Schoolites, Angels, Villains, Cobs and the more recognisable Dawsons and Bales, the latter two named after founders of the School in 1600.

The sports days in 1935 and 1936 were both somewhat of a washout due to thunderstorms, but in 1937 the weather was set fair, and Claude Banks was due to take part in the Under 12's 220-yard handicap. This race does not appear to have been handicapped, unlike some others, where participants are either recorded as 'scratch' or have a handicap of anything between two and 10 yards in this event.

This photo has long been lying in Dad's bureau, presumably it was too big to fit in any family photo albums and it was only the other day that I happened to turn the photo over and read on the reverse, in Dad's handwriting, *'P.W.Cole the winner, son of Thrapston Legion Secretary'*, and from newspaper reports of the day, R.N.Fountaine was 2nd and the very diminutive C.H.C.Banks was 3rd. The winner won in 30 seconds and two years later, in the Under 14's race, Dad again came third, with the winner clocking up 28 seconds.

220 yards seems a strange distance in today's metric age and it took me a while to work out (in old money) that 220 yards was one eighth of a mile, with 880 yards half a mile etc.

The newspaper reports always list the officials for the day and include a timekeeper. I cannot imagine the timing device used to record the times of these races, with some timings recorded as 11 and one-fifth seconds, 31 and four-fifth seconds and 61 and three-fifth seconds.

The connection with Mr T. R. Parker, school football coach, must have been a useful one as in March 1938 he brings his Southampton X1 to play a Kimbolton X1, where entrance was one shilling and I know that Dad was one of the boys watching, where they would shout "Play up the School".

There are two things I find particularly poignant about this story, one in the newspaper reports and the second in the photo. Reading the names of the winners, and runners-up in the races from the 1930's, I recognise many of the names as those read out by the Headmaster, at the War Memorial in the village on Remembrance Sunday as having lost their lives in WW2. Dad would always stand, during the two minutes silence, with tears streaming down his cheeks. From the playing fields of Kimbolton School – we will remember them.

Secondly, this tiny boy coming third, against much bigger boys. My youngest grandson, Henry, aged nine, came home from school the other day and said, "Nannie, I am the smallest person in my class, I am even smaller than all the girls". I told Henry that the most precious things come in small packages and that to me he is like the most valuable diamond ring, tiny but exquisite. Dad always remained small, and I think little Henry takes after him, but size is not everything and Dad's small stature certainly never held him back in life.

The Days of Sack Cloth and Ashes

Dad always called the days when the shooting season ended, as his time of sack cloth and ashes. How he would have hated shooting being stopped this season during lockdown. Only one shoot was held in October but still a magnificent bag of 101 was achieved. A sweepstake is always held before the day begins and every participant, whether 'guns' or beaters get a chance to win a share of the kitty for a £1 stake, with first, second and third prizes on offer. I always choose the age Dad would be now, (always hoping no-one has already bagged my number) so this year my 'bet' was 94.

Dad loved his shooting days, and his favourite format was finishing after the last drive, going home and getting his wet clothes off and enjoying a warm bath, (which he didn't normally like!) then going back out at around 7pm to a local pub, where they would sit down to a three course meal with wine or beer, and port to finish. Dad had by now packed up drinking, (it seemed to play havoc with his prostate!) and was quite happy with his glass of orange juice and lemonade.

The next day we would generally get a running commentary on the food. The meat was too tough, the vegetables had not been cooked enough, the gravy was too watery, the sherry trifle was not as good as his grandmother used to make! Dad was always brave enough to go where others feared to tread, by giving hostesses marks out of 10 for their sherry trifles!

The conclusion of Dad's favourite day's shooting would be the card school and in particular games of poker. They had so many different variations on the game of poker, which changed countless times over the evening, with the dealer of a new game choosing the rules for that game.

Dad must have been a rather good poker player and back in the day, he often would not get home until the early hours of the morning. I remember, as a child, coming down for breakfast one morning and the bread board which was always situated at Mum's end of the table, not quite lying flat on the table. The reason why became clear when Dad came in and did his 'ta da' moment, lifting up the bread board to reveal what looked like hundreds of pounds of mixed notes and coins in a massive pile; remember this was the days of 'ten-bob' and pound notes, but even so, I don't think us kids had ever seen so much money in our lives and even Mum seemed impressed!

I am now in *my* time of sack cloth and ashes. Strictly Come Dancing has finished for the season. Even after 18 series, I have not lost my love for this show and how it brightens our Saturday evenings from autumn through to just before Christmas.

As teenagers our parents were keen that we learnt to ballroom dance, as this was a skill we would need in our adult lives, at all the dances we would attend, and it was important that we knew the right steps. Sadly, we were at the cusp of those types of dances going out of fashion and discotheques and nightclubs were just coming into vogue. None the less, every Tuesday evening in the autumn, we would be dropped off at Pertenhall Village Hall for our ballroom dancing lessons, as our parents tried to push back the tide! There always seemed to be enough boys and girls to partner each other, so no same sex couples back then! We learned predominantly ballroom dances, so no Latin – Samba, Salsa or Tango, but we became quite proficient at the Waltz, Quick-step and Foxtrot. We also learnt group dances, (like an early day line-dance) and one in particular I remember dancing to, 'Son of my Father' by Chicory Tip, which always takes me back when I hear it on the radio now.

Then in early January a dance would be held annually at the Mandeville Hall, called 'The Nine to Ninety', where us kids could show off to our parents what we had learned at our classes and the grown-ups from the village and surrounding area would come and a wonderful evening was had by all. Our dance teacher brought along a stack of records and was up on the stage with his record player and would announce, "Ladies and Gentlemen, take the floor for a quick-step". We would all still be wracking our brains, thinking, oh goodness, what are the steps for this one whilst

Caldecote Manor Farm, Abbotsley 26ᵗʰ October 2012

L-R: Claude Banks, Joe Bates, Jeff Brown, John Bates, Robert Carress,
George Peck, John Saunders, Bob Banks (Claude's brother).

*I showed my sister this photo, to check on the names of a couple of the
guns. She looked at the date, on the reverse, and said that this could not
possibly be right – Dad looked so well. I checked the date, as I have all
dad's diaries and sure enough – that date – "Shooting at Caxton – be
at Joe's 8.15am". Dad had been seriously ill following an emergency
operation for colon cancer only four months before this picture was taken.
We had had the talk with the surgeon – 'the next 24 hours will be
crucial; we don't know if he will pull through' and here he is – glass of
sloe gin in hand and ready for a day's shooting. An amazing man.*

grown-ups would already be gliding around better than we
could ever learn how!

I think the dance I enjoyed most was the 'Gay
Gordons' and this always seemed to get everyone up on
their feet as the huge crocodile of dancers snaked their
way around the floor.

Us children filled the floor for our favourites, 'Simple Simon Says,' the Conga and the Okey Cokey and the adults were always up on their feet for the last dance, as Engelbert Humperdinck sang 'The Last Waltz'.

Come back soon Strictly, I am missing you already!

Big Strong Man (My Brother Sylvest)

At Huntingdon Races recently, the name of one of the horses stirred the memory of an old song that was sung in the pubs, when the beer had been flowing.

Incidentally the horse won, so I picked up a few bob and I have also been singing the song to my daughters and friends ever since, which I think they are enjoying!!

Have you heard about the big strong man?
He lived in a caravan.
Have you heard about the Jeffrey Johnson fight?
Oh, Lord what a hell of a fight.
You can take all of the heavyweights you've got.
We've got a lad that can beat the whole lot.
He used to ring bells in the belfry,
Now he's gonna fight Jack Demspey.
That was my brother Sylvest' (What's he got?)
A row of forty medals on his chest (big chest!)
He killed fifty bad men in the west; he knows no rest.
Think of a man, hells' fire, don't push, just shove,
Plenty of room for you and me.
He's got an arm like a leg (a ladies' leg!)
And a punch that would sink a battleship (big ship!)

It takes all of the Army and the Navy to put the wind up
    Sylvest'.
Now, he thought he'd take a trip to Italy.
He thought that he'd go by sea.
He dived off the harbour in New York,
And swam like a great big shark.
He saw the Lusitania in distress.
He put the Lusitania on his chest.
He drank all of the water in the sea,
And he walked all the way to Italy.
He thought he take a trip to old Japan.
They turned out a big brass band.
You can take all of the instruments you've got,
We got a lad that can play the whole lot.
And the old church bells will ring (Hells bells!)
The old church choir will sing (Hells fire!)
They all turned out to say farewell to my big brother
    Sylvest'.

For Auld Lang Syne

Kimbolton Cricket Club always seemed to be struggling for funds, and at the end of the Second World War they decided to hold an inaugural New Year's Eve Dance at the Mandeville Hall, which they hoped would become an annual event. Indeed, this one event, for many years, became the main fund raiser for the Club with monies raised on this night keeping the Club going for the whole of the next season. Tickets were printed, a band was booked, generally a three piece, a raffle was held and, by the 1960's, the redoubtable

Bill Haley was running the bar. This was a hugely popular event with people coming from all the surrounding villages and you needed to get your tickets early to avoid being disappointed. The numbers were swelled by several Scottish farming families who had moved into the area in the late 40's and early 50's. These native Scots certainly knew how to celebrate Hogmanay, as they called it, and very much added to the fun of the evening.

What brought these Scottish farmers down to our part of the world and when did they come? A little investigation was needed. It seems that many of them moved south during the 1920's and 1930's, when the whole world was going through a financial depression. Farming had been affected badly during this time which meant that land and bigger farms were available to buy in the east of England. The more benign climate and the lower average rainfall, (60 inches of rain on the West Coast of Scotland, compared to only 22 inches round here), were a great attraction. The Milk Marketing Board had been set up in 1933 and this gave dairy farmers a guaranteed income and therefore greater security. In the early days Norfolk, Suffolk and Essex would see the arrival of Pattersons, Alstons and MacMillans, but the later arrivals started moving into Hertfordshire and Bedfordshire, with names that are familiar to us in Kimbolton, such as Brodies, Lammies and Hunters. Indeed, the Brodies were comparative late comers, arriving at Tilbrook in 1950, where the whole family, all their belongings, plus their livestock, a herd of Ayrshire cows, came on a train at the cost of £340 for the lot!

Kimbolton Cricket Club New Year's Eve Dance had been going great guns, until two events, both occurring in late December, on consecutive years, made a huge hole in the fund-raising. The first was in 1967, when there was a serious outbreak of Foot and Mouth Disease. Suddenly a quarter of all tickets sold were returned, as the Scottish Farmers, and indeed any farmers with livestock, could not come off their farms and risk mixing with other farmers and pass on or catch this dreadful disease. I can remember Dad on the phone ringing round, trying to sell the spare tickets, but with mixed success. The Scottish contingent were sorely missed, there would be no 'Last Waltz' for them that year; Engelbert Humperdink's chart topping hit song which, for many years to come, was always the last dance of the night.

The following year, 1968, with ground to make up in the fund-raising stakes and with tickets selling well, the Cricket Club took another severe blow, as one of the worst flu epidemics, since the Spanish Flu of 1918, broke out and everyone was going down like flies. Mum and Dad both avoided getting the flu, but most members of the committee and general helpers were affected. However, the dance still went ahead, but with much reduced numbers.

The day after New Year's Eve, 1st January, was not a public holiday in those days and if that date happened to fall on a weekday, then it was a normal workday for most people. So, the big clear up at the Mandeville Hall the next day was left to Mum (Dad would not help, as this was 'woman's work'). Mum came home exhausted, took to her bed and did not get up again for 4-5 days. I don't know how we managed to eat, I am sure we had done the Christmas turkey to death by then, but as a family, we could chart Mum's decline in health to that time and she was never the same again.

The Racecourse – Kimbolton Races

Race meetings had been happening in Bedfordshire in the early 18th Century, with the first properly organised meeting in Bedford on a course known as 'Cow Meadow' between Elstow and Kempston in 1730. These were flat races, run over an oval course of around a mile in diameter.

By the early 1870's, whilst the race meetings in Bedford were well supported, they had become quite disorderly at times and had, to a large extent, degenerated into a mere reunion of professional betting men. New reforms and improved standards led by the Jockey Club and in addition new enclosed courses like Sandown Park and Kempton Park were attracting better horses and increased prize money and 1873 saw the last race in Bedford.

The Oakley Hunt had been established in 1800 and in 1861 they held their first race meeting or steeplechase. The races were initially held around the areas now known as Putnoe and Brickhill, but these were then fields owned by George Higgins. Over 400 equestrians turned up for this first meeting, which was professionally run, with the farm buildings providing stabling and a weighing room. The course crossed the road to Kimbolton at the bottom of Clete Hill and also included a water jump over a stream at the bottom. To add the level of entertainment, the stream had been dammed to increase the level of the water and a party of pedestrians, eager to see the horses leap over the water, crowded together on the side where the horses would approach the jump. A steward was engaged to drive the people back to allow the horses room to jump, when several spectators, unaware of the abrupt turn of the stream gradually backed up too far, until they found themselves in the water, up to their middles! The second year, instead of artificially deepening the brook, this time they widened it to a formidable 21 foot! 5,000 people turned up for this race meeting, with newspaper reports saying that the Oakley Hunt Steeplechases were becoming popular with all classes and not unlike today's 'ladies' days', a strong muster of beauty and fashion was assembled.

When Bedford began expanding and new houses were being built north of the town, the Oakley Hunt needed to find a new home for its annual race meeting.

In 1887 the Oakley Hunt Steeplechase moved to Kimbolton and was held here on and off until 1907, with the odd year missed out due to the War (Boer) or particularly unfavourable conditions. The Fixture was always held in March or April and with a little further investigation, would likely to have been held around Easter.

Local Masters of the Fox Hounds were stewards, along with a lot of gentry from the area, including, Lord Baring, Major Shuttleworth, Leopold de Rothschild, The Duke of Manchester and names we recognise today, Grey Duberley and George Farrer, with E. L. Welstead as the Clerk of the Course.

The course was not actually at Kimbolton, but at "Hoo Farm" at Pertenhall, held with kind permission of the owners. All races were run under National Hunt Rules and apparently it was a challenging course as far as the jumps were concerned.

The meetings in the 1890's were not riveting ones for the fixture, with variously poor crowds or low entries, but Mr

OAKLEY HUNT
STEEPLE CHASES.

UNDER NATIONAL HUNT RULES.

KIMBOLTON,

FRIDAY, APRIL 19th, 1901,

Over the " HOO," by kind permission of the Occupiers.

STEWARDS:

DUKE OF MANCHESTER.
LORD St. JOHN.
P. A. O. WHITAKER, Esq., M.F.H.
G. W. FITZWILLIAM, Esq, M.F.H.
GEO. EVANS, Esq., M.F.H.
C. WRIGHT, Esq. M.F.H.
CAPT. BROWNING.
H. WICKHAM, Esq.
R. ALSTON, Esq.
J. HILL, Esq.

CAMPBELL PRAED, Esq.
GRIFFITH JONES, Esq.
H. H. GREEN, Esq.
GREY DUBERLY, Esq.
B. D. COOKE, Esq.
GEO. FARRER, Esq.
B. KEPPEL, Esq.
J. ARKWRIGHT, Esq.
W. MILLS, Esq.
W. C. WATSON, Esq.

Judge : H. WICKHAM, Esq.,   *Starter :* CAPT. DALTON.

Clerk of the Scales : Mr. W. OVER.

Clerk of the Course and Stakeholder : E. L. WELSTEAD, Esq.,
Kimbolton House, St. Neots.

Saddle-Horses £1 1s.   Carriages 10s. each admission.

NOTICE TO OWNERS.—Owners desiring National Hunt Flat Race
Certificates must inform the Clerk of the Scales at the time of
weighing out, and sign a request to that effect.

The PUBLIC are particularly requested to enter and leave the Course
by the proper entrances, and not to break fences.

Race Card 1901

Oakley Hunt Steeplechases,

UNDER NATIONAL HUNT RULES,

KIMBOLTON,
MONDAY, APRIL 18th, 1892,

Over the "Hoo," by kind permission of the Occupiers.

STEWARDS.

DUKE OF MANCHESTER.
LORD St. JOHN.
LORD E. GORDON.
CAPT. BROWNING, M.F.H.
H. WICKHAM, ESQ., M.F.H.
CAMPBELL PRAED, ESQ.

J. CARBERY EVANS, ESQ.,
M.F.H.
R. ALSTON, ESQ.
H. MAGNIAC, ESQ.
H. ARKWRIGHT, ESQ.
J. HILL, ESQ.

Judge—CAPT. BROWNING.   *Starter*—Mr. T. TURNELL.

Clerk of the Scales—J. HILL, ESQ.

Clerk of the Course and Stakeholder—E. WELSTEAD, ESQ.,
Kimbolton House, St. Neots.

Carriages 10s. each admission.

The Public are particularly requested to enter and leave the
Course by the proper entrances, and not to break the fences.

Race Card 1892

Oakley Hunt Steeple Chase at Hoo Farm

Welstead was determined that the meeting would survive, and he and his team managed to get the funds together for the 1893 meeting where there was a large attendance. There was solid support from the local hunting community and house parties arranged by prominent patrons of the hunt contributed considerably towards the attendance.

These were race meetings as we would recognise today, with a starter, bookmakers, weighing room, jockey's silks, selling races and entries from horses which had run in the Grand National and jockeys with household names of the time.

The last meeting was held on 15th March 1907, and it seems that poor fields were the order of the day, with a walk-over for the Hoo Steeple Chase and only two horses facing the starter in the Hunt Cup. There were huge crowds on the day, in particular noted supporters of the Cambridgeshire and Oakley Hunts, but these were not enough to save the meeting.

*

I am pleased that I have been able to write the story for Dad. Being a keen race goer, I think he had an abiding fascination that one huge field, on land he once farmed, was called 'The Racecourse' and this is where the Oakley Hunt Steeplechases took place. Although the races at Hoo Farm had ceased long before Dad was born and even his father would only have been a small boy when they finished, Dad always knew exactly where the fences were on the course. He always told me that if he walked the land in a certain light of the day, perhaps early in the mornings or at dusk, he could see the shadow in the land, where the fences would have been.

'The End of me Old Cigar'

(1) Now it was several Christmas Eves ago,
The Landlord of The Star
Said here's a Christmas Box for you,
A ninepenny cigar.
I smoked it up to Easter when my dear devoted wife
Said "Why don't you throw the end away"
I said, "Not on your life".
Chorus:

Oh! The end of me old cigar
Hurrah Hurrah Hurrah
I strolled up Piccadilly and imagined I'm a star
And though I aint so handsome, I'm a bit of a la-di-da!
I tickle the ladies fancy with the end of me old cigar.

(2) Now I joined up for a soldier and overseas I went
You should have seen the German girls they fairly used the scent
But when the sergeant-major placed a tin hat on my head
I took it off him and said, "I'll wear it here instead".
Chorus:

(3) When I was a doctor, a lady came to me
She wanted vaccinating in a place you wouldn't see
But when I'd vaccinated her, you should have seen the scar
For I must have vaccinated her with the end of me old cigar.
Chorus:

(4) Then I took a trip to Paris, a Paris girl I met
We strolled along the boulevards, the boulevards we slept

103

She took my watch, she took my chain, she took them home to
*   her Ma*
But I'll see her in hell before she gets the end of me old cigar.
Chorus:

(5) Then I took a trip to Brighton and strolled along the shore
And there I thought I'd take a look, behind the coffee store
And there I saw a lady who had just been washed up on the shore
She had nothing on but seaweed, so I took another draw

*   At the end of me old cigar*
*   Hurrah Hurrah Hurrah*

The lady said "Sir, I don't know who you are
But I wish you'd give me something to cover my figure
So I gave her the band I had just took of the end of me old cigar

Chorus:

Oh! The end of me old cigar
Hurrah Hurrah Hurrah
I strolled up Piccadilly and imagined I'm a star
And though I aint so handsome, I'm a bit of a la-di-da
I tickle the ladies fancy with the end of me old cigar.

The End

Claude with guest, Clive Bates, at his shoot dinner. Claude in full-flow with a rendition of 'The end of me old cigar'. It's one of those 'musical hall songs' that just when you think surely this must be the final chorus – No! – Hoorah, Hoorah, Hoorah! – along comes another verse!

Out of the Blue

Just recently I had a pleasant surprise, when I was invited to attend the Hunts County Cricket Club Awards Evening and Dinner, held at The Wood Green Animal Centre near Godmanchester.

My daughters had perhaps got wind that I was going to be honoured and had arranged for friends and family to join us, making up a big table of guests.

We were treated to a delicious meal, where each course was interspersed with awards to young up and coming cricketers in the County.

Shortly before the guest speaker, David Steel, a player for Northants and England back in the 1970's, got up to entertain us with tales of his cricketing exploits, a new cricketing award, that of Lifetime Volunteer to Huntingdonshire Cricket was announced and I was to be the first recipient.

The citation read that from helping make Kimbolton Cricket Club a huge force in village cricket from the early 1950's, to serving on the Huntingdon County Cricket committee in various roles, from Secretary, to Chairman and President and for being the first manager of the Hunts Over 50's cricket team in the first season of this national competition.

I duly responded that my enjoyment in playing cricket from as young as 6 years of age until I was nearly 70, was reward in itself, but that I was hugely honoured to accept this award.

It was wonderful to see old pals such as Bev Bradford and Hughie Edwards of Ramsey, Vince Reed from Papworth and John Gillett of Waresley, where conversations turned to what had happened all those years ago, with dodgy umpiring decisions still fresh in the mind.

I now have a bright shiny cup sitting on the shelf to remind me of a wonderful evening, which I won't forget in a hurry.

Sadly, this was the last story Dad ever wrote. The Dinner he speaks about was at the end of November 2016 and Dad sadly passed away just 11 weeks later. The recipients of awards had all been given instructions, that in order to keep the evening flowing, acceptance speeches were to be no longer than five minutes. Dad had been writing his speech for days and when I read it, I could tell it would last half the evening! I told him that he was only allowed five minutes to talk, and that I would re-write it for him. All duly done and typed up in large writing. Dad got up to receive his award and in front of an audience of 150 people, with no notes, all from memory, Dad made the speech he had written out in the first place and all the evenings timings went right out the window! Dad was determined to have his last moment in the spotlight – and he did!

CHAPTER SIX

The Villages and its Characters

Jimmy Cook of Hoo Farm

The Cook family took over Hoo Farm at Pertenhall in 1912, having previously farmed at Haynes. The outgoing incumbent was a Mr Oliver, who was unlucky in that he was the only farmer in Pertenhall who had suffered from the disastrous hailstorm of Thursday 2nd August 1906. According to weather reports gleaned from the archives, he had 40-50 acres of cereals ruined at the tip of the farm, where the Pertenhall brook joins the River Kym. This storm had brewed up during a sultry afternoon and together with gale force winds and a continuous electrical storm, which had started between Woburn and Newport Pagnell and then tracked through East Anglia to the Wash. The harvest in Little Staughton and Keysoe Row was ruined almost beyond redemption and, but for a nationwide appeal for compensation, many farmers, small holders and agricultural workers would have been knocking on the workhouse door.

Jimmy's parents, William and Kate, who died in 1931 and 1935 respectively and were survived by sons James (Jimmy) and William and daughters, Kate, Alice, Esther and Ruth. A brother of William senior, known to everyone as Uncle Tom came with the family and as far as I am aware, had no financial interest in the business, but worked on the farm until he died.

The son William had a short life, dying at the age of 21 from pneumonia. The story goes that he was working with the other men, stooking the sheaves of wheat down near the Old Black Barn one day where it had been raining non-stop. He had no waterproof clothing and instead of going home to change at lunchtime, he carried on working and caught a chill which was to prove fatal.

Kate, the eldest daughter, became the primary school teacher at Pertenhall and was there when I started school in 1930. She was quite a firm teacher, but also very kind, which is important for children at that stage in life. She left the area to go back to Haynes to teach, sometime around the beginning of the War and remained a spinster, as did her sister Alice, who housekept for Jimmy (James) until he married. Ruth, the youngest daughter married Charlie James from Keysoe and Esther married a farmer from Raunds.

Jimmy carried on farming after his father died in 1931, until he himself died in 1970. Although the Lock family, who lived at The Manor in Pertenhall were very influential in the village, in my opinion, Jimmy's input into Pertenhall village life was the most important contribution of anyone during that time. Not only was Jimmy an excellent farmer, but he was also hard working as well as being a good neighbour, who would help anyone in need. He was one of the church wardens, captain of the cricket team and always ready to be M.C. at any functions that were held at the school.

When the War ended, the church, after years of austerity, was in a dreadful state of repair. Jimmy organised a game shoot along with Tom Bates and others during the autumn of 1945, with all monies raised to go to the church. Most able-bodied villagers turned out as beaters and Jimmy organised the team of guns. I wonder how much the church benefitted from the sale of game, but I am sure it was very substantial. The following year, Charlie Banks (Claude's Dad), Vic Banks and Oliver Whitlock of Lt Staughton formed a local shoot, based at The Crown public house and it is still going today, some 70 odd years later.

Jimmy loved his shooting, and his gun, pipe and dog were almost always his constant companions. He carried on farming right up until the end and gave up the few years of retirement just for his love of country life and shooting in particular. The view from the garden of Hoo Farm to the south and east is stunning, and it was even possible during the London Blitz to actually see the flicker of the explosions. I remember Jimmy telling me that during the wet year of 1953, the floods were out all along the Pertenhall brook on his land for 22 mornings. No talk of global warming back then!

The old saying, "Like dog, like master" is usually quite true, but in Jimmy's case, although he had many dogs in his time, none of them could match their master. His last dog was a golden Labrador bitch and not only was she good at retrieving game, but she had a nasty habit of starting fights among the other dogs and became very unpopular as a result. An earlier dog, a mongrel cross between a Labrador and a sheep dog had a complete mind of its own and lost one of its legs in an accident at harvest time. As soon as it recovered, it was out round the farm with Jimmy, and he trained it to run around the fields of sprouts and scare off the pigeons!

Jimmy was one of the first farmers to go all arable and as he grew sugar beet, sprouts, potatoes and other labour-intensive crops, he needed a large workforce to cope. At one time, Stan, Olly and Cliff Stapleton all worked for him, together with a couple of Reynolds who lived in one of the farm cottages and also Jack Waller, who married Molly Bennett and took over the secretaryship of the cricket club very conscientiously.

An amusing story emerged at around this time, where Jimmy's men were having their breakfast near the potato clamp and Jack sat at the end of the row. He had recently been fitted with new dentures, but they were giving him trouble when he was eating, so he took them out and laid them down beside him. Jimmy turned up plus dog, to check on how things were going, as was normal, and whilst the conversation was progressing, the dog picked up Jack's teeth and ran off with them!

It was a shame that Jimmy did not marry until late in life and his marriage was not blessed with children. He told me, about five years before he died, that in his father's Will, the farm had been left in equal shares between him and his four sisters. Jimmy was allowed a free hand to farm the land, but he must pay out his sisters before the farm became his own. For many years this must have seemed like a millstone around his neck, as farming until the War was hand to mouth at the very least. I wonder if this is the reason why Jimmy remained single, so that he could concentrate on paying off the farm. He had only just accomplished this when he was telling me the story and he then decided to re-equip his farm with some much needed machinery and carry on farming, mainly he said so that he could still run the shoot and continue to receive invitations back from his guests.

Jimmy had a good pal in Tom Bates and their wives got on well together. I think Jimmy was probably more married to his farm than to his wife, but as all round ability goes and for being a genuinely good man, he would get 10 out of 10 in my book.

The Roddis Family

William (Fubby) Roddis, a native of Pertenhall, married Emma Wildman, whose parents kept 'The Carpenters Arms' public house which was along the West End Road in Little Staughton, and this pub, together with so many old properties, have disappeared in the mists of time. Seven children came along from the marriage, Edward (Ted), Joe, Bill, Jeff, Victor, Bessie and Edith. One must wonder how the ends were made to meet, with the miserly amount farm workers were paid in those days; remember there was no family allowances or free school dinners to help out back then.

There was a barn with the property where they lived, which housed the wood, coal and bicycles and was a veritable 'Aladdin's Cave' of all hand tools needed for farm work and gardening, from hedge laying to thatching the straw stacks. A work bench with a vice and various lasts that enabled Mr Roddis to repair all the families' shoes. A large garden and an allotment were cultivated and supplied the family with year-round vegetables. Flower beds and lawns were luxuries that many could not afford for the loss of growing space, nor the time for relaxation, but the occasional rambler rose made a welcome splash of colour.

Most of the children's clothes would have been hand-made and passed down to the younger ones when grown out of. Nothing was wasted in those days and many old jacket or trousers were cut into strips and made into rugs. Mrs Roddis somehow found the time to act as caretaker for the village school, which entailed, as well as cleaning, lighting the fire at about seven o'clock in the morning, so the schoolroom was warm before the teacher and pupils arrived. It is certain that the few coppers she was paid for doing this chore would not have been frittered away.

Their home was the thatched cottage (still there) at the crossroads at Green End and was tied to Fubby's job at Manor Farm, Pertenhall. The rent money would have been covered by a few extra hours worked on a Sunday morning, feeding and milking livestock.

As the family grew up, Ted, Joe and Bill joined their father, working at Manor Farm. Ted and Joe married two sisters, Winifred and Edith Squirrel from Dean.

Winifred produced two sons, Peter, who spent all his working days at Manor Farm and married Mary Weller, whose parents had come to Pertenhall in 1937 as gardener and housekeeper for the Lock family. Peter can be considered particularly unlucky as he had put so much into 'life's pot', but when his time for retirement came, like many others around these parts, he was denied the pleasure of growing old peacefully. Peter had officially retired, but still did driving jobs for the Bates during busy times. He had taken a load of wheat to Whitworths at Wellingborough and whilst in the queue to tip the load, he had a massive heart attack and died in the cab of his lorry and it was only discovered when the queue stopped moving. Bob, the other son, was the same age as me and we are together in the school photograph in 1930, aged 4. Bob married Nel Filsell from Keysoe and also spent all his working life at Manor Farm and their son, David, now lives in Risely.

Joe and Edith's son, Jack, went to Kimbolton Grammar School and became a useful cricketer. He married Mary Hart from Tilbrook and moved away from the area.

Daughter Bess married Jabe Robins from Little Staughton and for around ten years after the War were landlords of 'The Kangeroo' pub, which became a hugely popular watering hole for many locals. Bess and Jabe by this time had produced two sons, Peter and Robert, the latter of whom was a demon fast bowler on local cricket pitches. Daughter Gladys who married an American serviceman and went to the States and produced 7 or 8 children. The other daughter, Edith, stayed closer to home and married Archie Breed from Bedford, where they set up home.

Jeff Roddis married Joyce Stringer, who was in service for Pelhams at Wood End House, and they went to live at Keysoe Row. Jeff was one of the first people in the village to own a motor bike and he went to work at the Igranic Engineering Works in Bedford and was one of the very few people at that time not to be involved in agriculture.

Victor Roddis (Vic) started working for Johnny Bates down Wood End Lane and went on to marry Joan Harris from Stonely. Joan had been an evacuee during the War, originally from Gt. Yarmouth. The marriage produced one son, Malcolm, who went to Kimbolton Grammar School. He was a most likeable young man, as well as being probably the best local fast bowler ever produced. When Malcolm left school, he was offered terms to join Northants County Cricket Club, but he turned it down to join the Manchester Police Force and in the early 1970's emigrated to Canada, initially with the intention of joining the Canadian Police Force, but shortly before he was due to sign up, another job offer came along and he became involved in the poultry feeding and egg processing industries, which took him all over the world. He recently retired from the egg processing industry.

Sometime during the 1920's and 1930's an outbreak of polio occurred and several children in the area were affected. Bill caught it probably worst of all and Jeff to a much lesser degree. It is difficult to imagine how the family coped in those desperate times and I can only imagine that hope and prayer were high on the agenda, together with the hard work that was part and parcel of life at that time.

When Bill grew up, just how he managed to do a job of work on the farm is almost beyond belief. Both his legs and his feet and his right arm were horribly disfigured, with his left arm the only unaffected limb. Yet with his sheepdog and a determination I have never seen before, or since, he worked with the livestock up until retirement.

If guts and strength of character were the yardsticks that determined the size of medals dished out, Bill would have been presented with one the size of a wagon wheel.

The expression "salt of the earth" could have been coined especially for the Roddis family. Their input into the working and social life of the village was immense. All the family have been very supportive of the church, from grass cutting, bell ringing, organ blowing and grave digging, in fact anything that needed doing.

*

Mary Roddis was always Dad's 'go to' person when he wanted to check facts for his stories, and they used to enjoy long chats on the phone reminiscing. The village lost Mary, aged 88, just four months after Dad in 2017. A packed church gave her a wonderful send off and back to The Manor afterwards for a wonderful tea on the lawns hosted by the Williams' family. Mary's wonderful smile and positive attitude will be missed, but a link to the Roddis family, all of them, Pertenhall through and through.

Pentenhall Womens Institute in Celebratory mode – possibly from VE Day 1945.

Back Row L-R: *Rene Presland, Vicky Jessop, Rita Holyoak, Mrs Packer, Mrs Cook.*

Middle Row: *Nora Bates, Mrs, Waghorne, Aunt Nell (Banks), Mrs Peppit, Edie Roddis,*
Mrs Weller, Miss Hartop, Grace Hardwick, Mrs Alec Bates, Mrs Robinson, (?), Sue Shelton, Mrs Lily Reynolds, Mrs Seal.

Front Row: *Joan Peppit, Mrs Holyoak, Freda Stapleton, Mary Weller, Lizzy Stapleton, Miss Modlen, Win Roddis, Molly Weller, (?) Miss Mable Wagstaff.*

The Unlucky Farm

Grange Farm, Pertenhall, for as long as I can remember, has been in the Shelton family. The farm qualifies for being known as 'unlucky' because it has seen more than its fair share of misfortune. Sid Shelton was the first incumbent and during the depression in the 1930's, kept a flock of hens, which provided Evans of Leicester with eggs to be hatched which were then sold as chickens. Sid lost two wives, before being wed to Sue of the Bates family. His first son, also called Sid, died in Bedford Hospital, aged just 12 years old, after complications set in after being kicked on his knee by a horse at harvest time. The boy had just completed one term at Kimbolton Grammar School.

In October 1939 the first two bombs dropped in Bedfordshire, fell on Shelton's farm, blowing out all the windows in the farmhouse and leaving huge craters in the fields. As schoolboys, me and my best friend, John Shelton went and collected up shrapnel from the bombs and sold the bits to the boarders at KGS!

The second wartime occurrence was when the RAF was preparing for the Dambusters raid on Germany. The Pertenhall valley was very similar terrain to what they were going to encounter during the raid on the Ruhr Valley and their low flying practising resulted in 15 foot being lopped off the elm tree near the road on the farm.

Lastly, for the wartime mishaps, was the story of the Italian prisoner which was told in *'Once a Man – Twice a Boy'*, where my friend, John Shelton, by then 18 years old and in the Home Guard, saved the day and was commended for his actions.

John's heroics did not end there, nor the misfortunes to befall this Farm. In another story recounted in my first book, John and his sister Sheila saved a mother and her son from drowning when the brook on the farm flooded, but sadly the little girl in the vehicle, which was swept away in the torrent, lost her life. John was awarded the British Empire Medal for his act of bravery.

Fast forward to the next generation, John's son David, always known as The Duck, almost lost his life after falling into a silo of rape seed. Were it not for the vigilance of the lorry driver and his quick thinking to switch off the machine and haul 'The Duck' out, this would have been another sad tale.

Chadwell Spring

Whilst Dad talked about the Chadwell Spring in many of his stories, he never got round to giving it a story all of its own, so I will hope to do it justice. I had done a tiny bit of my own research back in 2006, simply googling 'Chadwell Spring' and up came a list of 'Holy Wells and Springs of Bedfordshire'. These included Holywell, a village on the borders of Bedfordshire and Hertfordshire, near Hitchin. At Hail Weston there are mineral springs, formerly looked on as Holy Wells, but the waters were used by Paines, the brewery at St. Neots for their bottled mineral drinks. There were mineral springs and wells at Turvey (St. Mary's Well), Bromham and Cranfield. Back in ancient times and even up to the early 1900's, these waters were seen to have magical healing properties.

The list included Chadwell Spring, which is at Chadwell End and although Dad was born at Chadwell Farm, the spring was actually on his grandfather's farm, Manor Farm, Pertenhall. It was a sizeable spring and the water had been bottled at times over the years and was said to be good for sore eyes.

I asked Dad to take me there one day, as I wanted to see it for myself, imagining some huge 'water feature', like you see in a garden centre. So, we piled into his pick-up truck, and he drove me up to Pertenhall, down Green End and onto a piece of rough ground. He parked up and we got out. He then pointed out the Spring, but I could not see anything just the most enormous patch of brambles, like those that must have surrounded Sleeping Beauty's palace. You would not have been able to get within 15 feet of the Spring from any direction, such were the ferocity of the mass of briers. The water, I imagine, was bubbling up somewhere in the middle of these bushes and extremely fertile it must have made the soil, given the height and spread of these brambles. How disappointing, I was totally underwhelmed.

When Dad was in his first year at Kimbolton School, he collapsed one day and was taken to his grandmother's house in Kimbolton High Street. He had contracted scarlet fever, a very serious illness at the time, especially before antibiotics, and in many cases this proved fatal. The symptoms were a bright red rash, covering most of the body, with a sore throat and high fever. Probably, not unlike measles, Dad could not bear any light and was kept in a darkened room, with his grandmother gently sponging him with tepid water, to try and bring his temperature down. The doctor, from the surgery called daily, but Dad was not getting any better. He told Dad's father to go up to Chadwell Spring and bring fresh bottled water and try and get as much of it into him as they could. Eventually he began to recover. Dad's grandmother now needed to start to feed him up to get his strength back. She asked Dad what he liked to eat, to try and whet his appetite and he told her that he liked a pork chop. Every day she went to the butcher and brought him a fresh pork chop. It was six weeks before Dad was strong enough to go back to school. He very nearly had to learn to walk again.

The legacy of this was, Dad would never eat another pork chop again, he couldn't stand the sight of them! So, if Dad did not eat pork chops, that meant we did not get served pork chops either! During the school holidays, it was always a treat for us kids to go to play with cousins for the day and we especially liked going up to Pertenhall. One such day we were at the Bates (where the Chadwell Spring is) and we were called in for lunch. Auntie Elizabeth had cooked us pork chops with all the veg and gravy. Never having eaten these before, I cut into the very thick golden rind on the pork chop, thinking it was a roast potato and popped a huge piece into my mouth. Oh my goodness, it was horrible, oozing hot fat running down my throat, I thought I was going to gag! I do not know how I managed to finish the mouthful, but somehow must have done, leaving the rest of the rind, but eating everything else, which was delicious. I have to say, like Dad, I am not a massive fan of pork chops, but for a different reason!

Everything in it's Time

When the shooting season gets underway, this timely poem is always worth an airing. Although 12th August sees the start of the grouse shooting, followed by partridge shooting in September, October is always the month I look forward to – the start of the pheasant shooting.

January brings the snow,
makes our feet and fingers glow.

February brings the rain,
Thaws the frozen lake again.

March brings breezes loud and shrill,
which stirs the dancing daffodil.

April brings the primrose sweet,
Scatters daises at our feet.

May brings flocks of pretty lambs,
Skipping by their fleecy damns.

June brings tulips, lilies, roses,
Fills the children's hand with posies.

Hot July brings cooling showers,
Apricots and gillyflowers.

August brings the sheaves of corn,
Then the harvest home is borne.

Warm September brings the fruit,
Sportsmen then begin to shoot.

Fresh October brings the pheasants,
Then to gather nuts is pleasant.

Dull November brings the blast,
Then the leaves are whirling fast.

Chill December brings the sleet,
Blazing fires and Christmas treats.

And Finally...

My thanks to all at Troubador, especially to Hannah Dakin and Beth Archer, who have held my hand all the way through the process, even when things weren't going smoothly!

To Emma at The Framery (www.theframery.co.uk) – they are so much more than just picture framers. Emma can make the oldest photos (and some of them are!) look like they were taken yesterday – so thank you Emma and Andy!

To my very good friend and often mentor, Dr Gareth Thomas, for his belief in my writing ability and storytelling. For often pushing me well beyond my comfort zone, for reading my stories, suggesting improvements, writing the forward to the book and the back cover notes and for helping me with proof reading – often the author does not see their own mistakes!

To the readers of the 'Bystander', our local monthly magazine, for their very kind comments and encouragement, which is often all I need to carry on writing and help keep Dad – Claude's memory alive.

 Matador